"What you are is God's gift to you,
what you become is your gift to God."

— Hans Urs von Balthasar, *Prayer*

THE GIFT

Kendall P. Geneser

concordispublishing.com

First Concordis Publishing Softcover edition March 2023

DESIGNED BY RODNEY V. EARLE

Manufactured in the United States of America

10 9 8 7 6 5 4 3 2 1

ISBN: 979-8-218-17843-7 (Softcover)
ISBN: 978-8-218-17845-1 (eBook)

Contents

Foreword

A decade ago, I did not fully comprehend the level of adversity on the path before me. I failed to recognize the degree of difficulty facing those around me, as well. Yet, as things progressed—thus far slowly, thankfully—I began to recognize the simple grace, the stalwart determination, and the unspoken kindness of the splendid fellow human beings all around me. And rather than curse an untenable circumstance, I choose to focus on that narrow strip of light out there on the horizon.

Initially, as I heard more about my future, I was certain that I wouldn't live to see my children grown, much less hold my first grandchild. Within hours, as I learned more about my diagnosis, I became convinced that this would not severely impact my life. I was dreadfully wrong on both counts. The wild gyrations of my rather hyperactive pendulum finally settled with some sense of equilibrium. I think.

Ten years after being diagnosed with multiple sclerosis (MS), I can assure you that what I thought I knew then was, at first, woefully pessimistic, then woefully optimistic, ultimately settling on realistic and mostly upon uncertainty. In other words, the more I learned, the less I knew. I can tell you one thing that is certain, though: somewhere tomorrow, it will be sunny. I can see it by that thin strip of the horizon.

This I know: if your life is anything like mine, you have neither the time nor the inclination to read someone else's drivel. With that in mind, I will try to keep the bullshit to a minimum. Having promised to limit any streams of consciousness and realizing that my next comment probably confirms that I am delusional, you might find something to latch on to here. That is why I choose to tell my story; that and this effort affirms my therapeutic intention to step out of the closet.

INTRODUCTION

The Gift came into being as a self-published novella-sized memoir a long time ago. It attempts to explain the trials and tribulations that I faced when—at age thirty-four—I was diagnosed with Multiple Sclerosis. The work documents my reaction and response throughout the early years of my disease and culminates with my stem cell transplant some ten years later. During those early years, I figured that perhaps my disease was not the end but merely the harbinger of something bigger, more important, than that of a naval aviator.

This therapeutic endeavor lacks the tidy conclusion that I had originally envisioned. That is because when I ended *The Gift,* I understood that Multiple Sclerosis was indeed a harbinger of something bigger. Yet, I did not comprehend that it was the catalyst of strange and wonderful alchemy whose effects reverberate to this day.

As a consequence, one is left a bit wanting when they read the words THE END. Though aptly titled, it has taken me another decade to discover exactly what that priceless gift represents.

I liken the effort to describing the color of the sky to someone who is blind. When finished, one realizes that something is missing, lost in translation. While *The Gift* is a compelling story, it needs closure.

Grounded: A Different Kind of War (my newly-released memoir) was originally intended as an update for readers of *The Gift*. The two stories—written independently of one another—make up the arc of one tale and reveal, I believe, the true author. That is the ultimate closure.

THE GIFT

Kendall P. Geneser

CHAPTER ONE
A Warrior's Heart

I wanted to be somebody. Somebody you'd know, a name you might drop casually at a cocktail party, and having done so, whisk back to the bar to freshen your martini, leaving a passel of duly impressed partygoers in your wake. But alas, I'm nobody. Back then, I perceived—perhaps a wildly optimistic sentiment—that I was on the path to, if not greatness, at least recognition. I did not know it then, but my path had a huge speed bump.

A line from Stanley Kubrick's film *Full Metal Jacket* says something to the effect of, "I just wanted to be the first kid on my block with a confirmed kill." Well, in a word, that was me. The guy who delivered that line was a heartbreaking, life-taking Marine, played by an eternally youthful Matthew Modine. I wasn't a part of the USMC but instead a naval aviator (now medically retired). I never wanted to be a Blue Angel, a test pilot, or even an astronaut. Though they are all laudable goals, those noble and even logical next steps never really interested me. First, because I am not smart enough to tackle the rigorous academics necessary to achieve the latter, and second, because I never wanted to be away that much (they consider nine months out of a year as a Blue Angel as a shore tour). I just wanted to be a fighter pilot. Not just any fighter pilot. I wanted to be a really good one. Not in other people's eyes, necessarily, but in my own. Before you consider me to be some sort of psycho, please note that were it not for a few million citizens with rather aggressive mindsets such as my own, you might be reading this in some other language right now. Sprechen sie Deutsche?

Thankfully, and in some sick way, regrettably, I never enjoyed the terrible burdens of legitimate combat. Alas, many of my contemporaries and vast numbers of active duty and reserve personnel cannot say that today. And, regrettably, more than a few have paid the ultimate price. For those people, both the living and the dead, regardless of one's political bent, we should get down on our knees every day.

As for me, personally, I joined the U.S. Navy on June 23rd, 1985, as part of the multitude of wannabes flocking to President Reagan's call for a 600-ship navy. Upon my graduation from William Penn College in May, and after marrying my wife in June, I gained acceptance into Aviation Officer Candidate School. As a consequence, my new bride spent all of her honeymoon—incidentally, she doesn't call it that—in Pensacola, Florida, much of it alone. I owe her for so many things.

Since that time, I have managed to drag her across the globe gleefully. We have lived—well, actually, she lived, and I just visited when ashore—in Florida, Texas, California, Japan, and Nevada. And though she doesn't ever let me forget her many trials and tribulations along the way, secretly, as the recruiting commercials used to say, I think she considered the burdensome task of being a naval officer's wife "not just a job, but an adventure." More important, some might say, amazingly, we're still happily married. Who woulda thunk?

I got my wings on December 17th, 1987. We were assigned to Naval Air Station Miramar in San Diego, CA, to fly Tomcats (F-14s). After time in Japan (I was a Black Knight in Fighter Squadron 154 in the fleet), we eventually found ourselves at Naval Air Station Fallon, Nevada. Why is there a navy base in Nevada? It was a remnant of World War II. It was once one in a string of dots on the map denoting a line in the sand meant to quell a Japanese onslaught that never came.

It later became the place where naval air forces still do their overland training. I thought it was an intermediate stopover, a run-of-the-mill shore tour, the chance to catch our breath before our Department Head Tour, but it ultimately proved to be the place where my—what was slowly shaping up to be a decent—career came to an abrupt end.

I was nearing the end of a tour as an aggressor/instructor pilot in the now-defunct Strike Fighter Squadron 127 (VFA-127). I had transitioned to Hornets (F/A-18s) and had orders to NAS Lemoore, California, when I went for a jog on Thanksgiving morning, 1995. Intent on spending much of the afternoon stuffing my face, I dutifully ran a few miles to counterbalance my gluttonous tendencies. Upon my return, I noted a strange tingling sensation on the entire right side of my body. From head to toe, I felt it grow in amplitude as the day wore on. It wasn't painful in any way, just weird.

I thought nothing of it, but when I went back to work the next day, I mentioned it to our flight surgeon in the debriefing. He had flown with me in an empty backseat, a 2v2 against the Fleet Replacement Squadron (FRS). It was somewhat ironic that my passenger happened to be our squadron's doctor—also unusual since all but one of our airplanes were of the single-seat variety.

A month earlier, he had diagnosed similar tingling (this time only in my left leg) as sciatica and said I should stop doing things that might aggravate it. He suggested that I should stop running, stop lifting weights, and, if possible, stop flying. I had responded by submitting to the first two conditions (indeed, the run on Thanksgiving morning had been my first in nearly a month) but explained that I wouldn't stop flying unless grounded. How prophetic of me.

On this day, November 30th, 1995, my exact words were, "Hey, Doc, I got this sciatica thing back. This time it's on the whole right side of my body."

With those words, he knew that we weren't talking about back pain. Sciatica doesn't work like that, but back then, who knew?

"Why don't you stop by my office this afternoon?" he asked casually.

I waved him off, still oblivious. "I'd like to, but I got another 'hop' this afternoon."

"No, you don't," he said. That was the last time I ever flew an ACM (air combat maneuvering) hop. Then and there, my career as a naval aviator effectively ended.

I spent the next year of my life trying to get back in the cockpit. Meanwhile, VFA-127, about to decommission, hurriedly "cut" orders for me to report over to NSAWC (the Navy Strike and Air Warfare Center) across the street while I considered my medical options.

Jackie Waldman, author of *The Courage to Give* and *People With MS With the Courage to Give* counted among her works, inspired me, though I doubt she realizes it, to author this story. She refers to living with MS as a "new normal." Well, in short, my acceptance of that new normal was slow in coming. In 1995, 1996, and most of 1997, I was still operating under the "old normal." I still wanted to fly jets, and I would've gladly given my firstborn (sorry, Nick) or my left nut to do it.

There was something about flying pointy-nosed go-fasts, screaming over the desert so low that the sagebrush starts to look like trees, having truck drivers look down at you as you rip past at five or six bills. And I haven't even talked about flying around the boat, which is a lifetime of excitement compressed into fifteen seconds. I have heard people who do that kind of work describe it as "the most fun you can have with your clothes on." I would say that's a fairly apt description.

CHAPTER TWO
Diversions

I am the happy idiot, the court jester that happened to fly airplanes acceptably well. My squadron mates generally liked me. I am not sure if it was pity or resigned indifference, but generally speaking, I was thought harmless. But I am here to tell you that is not exactly the case. The truth is—though I myself am not even certain of this—that I might have been extremely dangerous in an actual shooting war. Happily, we will never know for sure. While I choose to consider myself an untested warrior, deep down, I will always wonder.

ACM (air combat maneuvering) is, like most endeavors, a blend of art and science. The truth is that it is a whole lot more science. Good fighter pilots do a few basic things very, very well, and according to the book, that is to say, according to lessons "written in blood."

Unfortunately, I do not possess the same wiring design as most fighter pilots. I believe I am right-brain dominant. Most good fighter pilots have a slight to severe dominance in the left hemisphere. I should have been a painter. Or an actor. Or a musician. Doctors tell us that the right side of our mind tends to be the more creative, artistic side, while the left hemisphere is more logical and quantitative.

For me, the sky was my canvas, the airplane my brush. Sometimes I wowed my opponents with seemingly impossible maneuvers. Other times I looked incredibly stupid when the impossible stroke of genius that I was trying to conjure turned out to be just that, impossible. More often than not, people who paint or fly by the numbers kick the living shit out of the people who like to color outside of the lines.

I kept telling myself that the combat was not real. I wanted to explore the outer limits and expand my repertoire. Yet, despite myself, I managed to become a decent "Nasal Radiator." I always told myself that in actual combat, I would straighten up and fly right. I would conduct my craft following the laws of physics. I would make quick work of any enemy bold enough to challenge an airplane with U.S. markings (there are not many, as aerial combat seems a thing of the past. Now, the bad guys just blow themselves up). I was probably fooling myself, though, because the fact of the matter is, you play the same way you practice.

It was beautiful, though, flying and fighting jets. It combines the visual cornucopia of every conceivable color in the spectrum along with the artistic grace of dance but on a dance floor fashioned by God. It is so beautiful that I felt it was high time that someone should try to share the experience with earthbound mortals, poor bastards. I decided I wanted to write about it. Of course, in my ignorance, I discounted the notion that other skillful writers had tried to capture the joy of flight long before me. Isak Dinesen's *Out of Africa* comes close but still misses. In my opinion, human language cannot capture the wonders of flight. I'm still trying.

How many fighter pilots have you ever known that aren't satisfied with their day jobs? I have known few—damned few, but I was their chief. I suppose it is the creative side of my brain constantly prodding me to that seemingly greener pasture on the next hill. But when other junior officers were bringing books to read on cruise, I decided to try and write one. There were several things wrong with the plan, but you've got to admit it was bold, in a blissfully ignorant sort of way.

In short, then, my quest to illuminate the utter joys of flight prodded me to become a writer. I finished my first manuscript around the time of my diagnosis. Point of order here: as of *this* writing, I'm still unpublished. I will retain my day job as long as MS allows. Having said that, I've been writing off and on since age twenty-five.

People often ask me about my hobbies. Well, along with reading, you're looking at it. While I once considered myself an outdoorsy, athletic sort—I used to camp and fish and hunt, was a four-sport letterman in high school, and team co-captain of the varsity baseball squad in college—MS has bound me to this new life. It is a life I have come to love. I used to fly jets and land them on ships, and that was really, *really* cool. Now I am a writer, and, I kid you not, that is even cooler.

CHAPTER THREE
Good Luck, Buddy

The next day I was Reno-bound. Washoe Medical has an excellent hospital, probably the only one large enough to justify an MRI machine in Northern Nevada. It was simple for the Navy to order an MRI, despite the expense, since they could easily justify it by measuring its cost against the cost of the equipment I flew. Furthermore, fighter jocks are worth millions in terms of the amount Uncle Sam invests in training one.

"This is simply precautionary," the flight doc said. "It will more than likely turn out to be nothing," he added unconvincingly.

I was too clueless to even be in denial. Needless to say, I did not recognize the doctor's concern. I just assumed that's exactly what the results would show. I would be granted a clean bill of health and be back on the flight schedule tomorrow. This would be nothing more than a lovely drive through the desert.

For those of you that have never had one, MRI (magnetic resonance imaging) technology was a relative godsend for those in the business of trying to diagnose multiple sclerosis. Before MRIs, a spinal tap gave the only irrefutable evidence of MS. At issue is that spinal taps don't always correctly identify the disease. Just a month later, mine was clean. In the hands of someone who knows what they're looking for, an MRI eliminates any guesswork.

The cacophony of metallic pings is somewhat grating on the active mind. The confines of the gadget are often quite unnerving for those that are even slightly claustrophobic. No one has ever accused me of having an active mind, and so long as I can breathe, cramped spaces don't bother me. Bottom line: I soon fell fast asleep with Garth Brooks blaring in my headphones.

While I slept, the MRI machine created several images of my brain, one slice at a time. The end products are several images of the brain and/or spinal cord that show any signs of what the doctors benignly refer to as enhancement. I forgot to mention that at some point, technicians inject you with a dye called gadodiamide or "gad" that enhances any hot spots or lesions, the telltale sign of an ongoing exacerbation.

Of course, I know a lot about MS today, subtle things that even neurologists cannot fully understand. But back then, I had a nice drive through the high desert, caught a nap, and was sent off with a handshake for yet another relaxing drive. The tech handed me the films, shook my hand, and, looking like he was about to bawl, said haltingly, "Good luck, buddy."

KENDALL GENESER

CHAPTER FOUR
Join the Club

There are more than four hundred thousand MS patients in the United States alone. Estimates range as high as 2.5 million worldwide. I didn't know it yet, but those numbers were about to increase. Meanwhile, the MRI technician's all too earnest "Good luck, buddy" had my mind racing. The sentiment was genuine, I'm sure. After all, I had strolled in the mighty warrior but had left a mere mortal.

Moreover, he was looking me squarely in the eye when he handed me the very film that he knew would lay me low, end my career, radically change my life, and change everything. After his comment, which was not quite as subtle as a fart at a wedding, even a social idiot like me recognized that the news was probably not good. Just how bad? My ordinarily dormant wasteland of a brain had ample room to run, and run it did. I spent the next sixty to seventy miles back to Fallon, imagining the worst. So much for the pleasant drive in the desert.

Upon my return, just after midday, I called my flight surgeon, who had already read the results via fax.

"You've seen the results?"

"Yes, I have. You need to stop by as soon as possible, and you may want to bring your wife."

As soon as he said the "you may want to bring your wife" part, I thought I had a terminal brain tumor or Amyotrophic Lateral Sclerosis (Lou Gehrig's Disease) and that I was bound to be pushin' up daisies within a year. I was numb, dazed, and confused. I was too numb to cry. Still, this whisper-thin wisp of logic reminded me that there wasn't anything to weep about just yet. So far, I knew nothing. Tears were for later.

Outside the medical facility, my wife, Sherri, and I sat in the car, attempting to drum up the courage to take our medicine. It was ours, not just mine. If you have ever been married, do you remember the part about "in sickness and in health?" Nobody thinks he or she will ever have to test the concept. People don't realize the enormity of those words, or if they do, they choose to bury their heads in the sand. I know I did. Thank God one of us was listening and took it to heart.   When you're young and strong and beautiful, they're just words, but there it is. It can happen. It was about to happen to us.

"I hope it isn't too bad. I just want to live long enough to see our kids grow up," I whispered, shedding a tear on my wife's shoulder as I said it.

We walked right in. No waiting if you're really sick.

"Have a seat," the doctor gestured. "I don't know how to say this, but I've read your results."

"And?" we both prompted simultaneously.

"It's MS. You've got multiple sclerosis."

I was a bit relieved. I had assumed that it was something that was bound to kill me shortly, but I knew a guy back home who had lived for years with MS. Yet, I still assumed that this disease was, in fact, terminal, though over a much more extended period. The one guy I knew that had it died when he was in his fifties or sixties. I know it kills the suspense, and for those of you who already suffer from MS, you probably already know this, but it's not terminal.

Still, on December 1st, 1995, I assumed I'd be dead in twenty years—maybe less. My doctor did little to assuage this fear since he knew only a little more about MS than me. I knew nothing. Not one damned thing. Up until this point in my life, I might have sneaked a second glance at those people. Might even feel a pang of sympathy, might grimace slightly, and think too damned bad for them. Yet, I did not want to make a scene. I sensed then and now know that people like that—people like me—do not want pity. I know that because now I am one among their number. People who walked around me with canes or people who used wheelchairs were simply non-entities to be ignored. I am a little more empathetic these days.

CHAPTER FIVE
MS

Twenty-four hours later, after considerable research—he didn't know much about MS, but he's a good person and even a good doctor—the doc called me, and in a sleep-deprived voice, recounted his research.

"Upon further review, multiple sclerosis is not deemed terminal. There are a lot of unknowns, but it's thought to be an autoimmune disease. I was wrong about that terminal part. It's not," he added once again, just to make sure I heard the relatively good news. He went on with a rather good description of the disease while I quietly exhaled. "It's thought to be an autoimmune disease. Generally, Crohn's, lupus, type 1 diabetes, psoriasis, and rheumatoid arthritis are all considered part of the autoimmune family."

That very afternoon I began my first regimen of IV steroids. Part of me, indeed a tiny part, thinks that it should be a requirement for all men to do a regimen of Solumedrol at some point in their lifetime, a requirement similar to a Muslim's pilgrimage to Mecca. Why do I say this? I think it should be part and parcel of every male's rite of passage because it is bound to make him more empathetic toward women suffering the effects of PMS.

Right about now, guys everywhere are shouting TURNCOAT, or worse, as books collectively slam shut. Solumedrol, the IV version of Prednisone, in massive doses, makes you irritable and makes you feel alternately euphoric and then depressed. You get cramps. You gain weight. I gained fourteen pounds the first time. You retain water like a sponge. I'm no rocket scientist, but what's that sound like? I've only done it a handful of times. As I understand it, it's a bit more intense than PMS, but it doesn't happen monthly, either. Again, I say I've only done intravenous steroids four, maybe five times in my life! Since three out of four MS patients are women, perhaps I should defer further comment as I lack credibility. I will say this, though; going through that just once will build a lifelong modicum of respect.

Why are steroids recommended for multiple sclerosis? These agents are essentially anti-inflammatory drugs. To understand how they work, allow me to digress for a moment. For fellow MS patients, who undoubtedly know this, kindly bear with me for a bit. The human brain contains nerve cells called neurons. Encasing each neuron is a coating or insulation called myelin. In MS (no one knows precisely why yet), antibodies turn on the body itself and attack the myelin.

As a consequence, the myelin sheath (as it's called) suffers damage. If that damage is severe, the neuron may become cut. In either case (cut or damaged), it's difficult, if not impossible, for the neurons to correctly transmit nerve impulses.

The hypothesis is that during periods of exacerbation, the damage is less if swelling around the damaged area is reduced. Having experimented with both the stick-your-head-in-the-sand-and-hope method and the proactive approach, that of utilizing one of the corticosteroids at the first signs of exacerbation, I, like most of the rest of the modern world, am a staunch supporter of early intervention. It works.

Why, in God's name, would you not do everything possible to delay the onset of the disability? Some asshole once told me that steroids were only treating the symptoms, not the disease itself. While technically that is, in fact, true, a bigger asshole bought it hook, line, and sinker and then failed to get the point. After all, if the disease will progress at its own pace, what's the point of fighting the symptoms? The point is—it only took me a decade to figure out the rest of the explanation—if you fight tooth-and-nail to delay the progression of disability a few years down the trail, you're less disabled than if you had done nothing. Essentially, in the early stages of MS, that is what I did: nothing; makes one want for a do-over. But there aren't any do-overs in this life. Weapons in your scabbard include IV steroids. Using them isn't a cure, but they do help.

CHAPTER SIX
A Head in the Sand

Of course, part of my reluctance to use IV steroids has been my personal battle with denial. It started early and was unwittingly aided and abetted by medical professionals in the U.S. Navy. The Department of Defense is not anxious to ground someone on whom they have spent millions of dollars. I am not insinuating that the medical profession finds it distasteful to end someone's career should the tenants of sound medicine dictate such a course. But what was obviously MS could have been something else. A litany of possibilities was explored and subsequently discarded as my level of disability marched steadily, almost imperceptibly, onward—Lyme disease for all my friends.

With the benefit of hindsight, despite the Hippocratic Oath, it becomes blatantly clear that doctors find themselves under extreme pressure from all sides. In what is arguably a unique situation, with management (the Navy) and labor (me) singing the same tune—that is, keeping me in the cockpit—doctors find themselves in a dreadful predicament. While most, if not all, will tell you that they do not give a damn about the Department of Defense where a patient's welfare is concerned, recognize that even these physicians (a vast majority) are under extreme pressure. They have to walk the tightrope of maintaining a patient's physical health while coddling his or her rather fragile mental stability. Since I used to derive and define myself out of what I did, and to a lesser extent, still do, delaying any official diagnosis—I'm guessing this—was perceived as necessary. So almost two years passed, with me hanging my hopes on it being something else. When asked questions like, "Does anyone else suffer from MS in your family?" The answer was always, "No, I'm the lucky one."

Recall that I wanted to get back in the cockpit. I still wanted to strap on a jet and bend it around a cloud. In other words, I had some difficulty accepting this harsh new reality, and the docs, in their infinite wisdom, slowly coaxed me toward the correct decision. It took great patience on their part. Seeing the writing on the wall was difficult. I'm not as smart as I look. I was officially diagnosed in the summer of 1997, almost two years after my first exacerbation.

Meanwhile, I actually did get to fly again. For the next year ('95–'96), I tried to get the doctors to give me the "omni-omni" and grant me full flight status, which they eventually did. I flew Hornets a little for nearly a year in 1996–97. But I knew. I knew one night after a flight when I went to sign "the book" (the Aircraft Maintenance Logbook), and my handwriting was different. It was actually a little better, but looking at it, it looked as though someone else had signed my name. I'm not a doctor, but I knew that wasn't good.

I eventually asked for a reevaluation. During the interim—I like to refer to it as my "limbo period"—MS, though largely inactive, was left to its own devices. The military medical profession's doorstep is not where the blame should be placed but instead should be caked squarely upon the shoulders of the guy driving the bus. The patient. Me.

KENDALL GENESER

CHAPTER SEVEN
Not Just a River in Egypt

Living in denial of one's circumstance is a double-edged sword. It can work for a disciplined master, but in the hands of a novice, it is an unruly beast that bites. Hard. Denial, when appropriately used, can enable us to ignore little obstacles or inconveniences. As an example, I've had MS for almost a decade, and I don't use a cane—at least publicly—yet. Sometimes, I'll admit I need a wheelchair, but I believe that in some ways, my very denial has prevented me from accepting this new reality, and, as a consequence, I'm still ambulatory, sort of. I've seen neurologists look on in amazement as I negotiate a hallway, mostly unaided.

Before you explode from your seats to give me a "standing O," read on. The other side of the blade is that my denial prevents me from enjoying a myriad of activities simply because I'm too proud to use a cane or a walker, or a wheelchair. I haven't come to grips with the idea of letting people know I'm now a klutz. Good friends would say at this point, "We didn't need a cane to tell us that you're a klutz." This self-imposed isolation is the result of two things. First, it's because I want to keep my disability a secret—with this effort, I'm busting out of my self-imposed closet—and second, the reason I'm in there in the first place is that I choose to deny my present reality.

As you can see, I'm still, after nearly a decade, wrestling with my own demons. The disease, however, progresses at its own pace. It doesn't give a damn about personal demons, and it can take all of you all at once. Or it can progress slowly, sometimes so slowly it cannot be measured. Thankfully, in my case—who knows what will happen tomorrow—mine seems to be moving at a rate that allows my mind, which is also advancing slowly, to comprehend this ever-changing state of being.

What this has allowed is that I'm slowly, though at an increasing rate, letting the world see and know me, MS and all. I haven't gotten there quite yet. I'm still a novice. As I pen these words, I know I'm still fighting with some denial. I'm not planning to use my cane at work just yet.

CHAPTER EIGHT
Criminal Intent

I don't know about the rest of you folks "in the closet," but it's a damned dark and kind of slimy way to live. It makes you feel like a criminal. Secrets of any kind are highly corrosive things. After a while, lying becomes second nature. You actually have a wee bit of pride in contriving some elaborate tale about that old football injury to explain away a limp.

Where I work now, there's an ample open space where the traders of energy and natural gas sit. Sometimes, when things are slow, one of the fellows on the floor will toss a Nerf ™ football around. I don't worry too much about it because I sit far away at the opposite end of this open area.

I only have to "run the gauntlet," so to speak, if I have to relieve myself. The "head" is down there. As I traverse the danger zone, I'm praying—praying, mind you—that I won't drag a foot and trip and, almost as crucial, that I won't see a ball come spiraling toward me. I was an athlete in college, but MS does not care about your résumé. It has no compunction about making you (read: me) look like an uncoordinated spaz. That is why I hope and pray that when I have to piss, no one will throw the ball at me. You cannot hide a lack of coordination.

There is something inherently wrong with that mode of thought. Why do we think hiding is necessary? But, if I were a company, I wouldn't hire me. Assuming full disclosure concerning my condition, I would look for some way to squirm out of hiring me or anyone with MS. The apparent reason is that hiring someone with a progressive disease has a reasonably precipitous downside. I know all about the Americans with Disabilities Act. It's a good thing. With it in place, lying is sanctioned. The problem is it is still lying. But, you say (incidentally, I say it too), I just want a job, and nobody will hire me if I tell the truth. I could go on and on with the argument that disabled people have with themselves daily. After all, don't we have a right to fair and equal treatment? I don't want to lie, but isn't telling the truth selfish in a way? Doesn't that put my family at greater economic risk? And who wants to be around someone who complains all the time, anyway?   Suck it up.   Don't we all have problems of some sort?

"You shall know the truth, and the truth shall set you free." My ass. It'll set you free, all right. You'll be unemployable. Yet the reality is that telling someone you limp because you injured your anterior cruciate ligament when you were a strong safety in high school—please don't think I just made that one up—is a blatant lie. I argue with myself all the time about things like this, saying, 'No, it's just stretching the truth a bit.' The fact is I did injure my ACL playing high school football, and, yes, it was at strong safety.   According to any competent orthopedist, I have a partial tear, and I never forget that it's there, but it's not why I limp. I limp because I have MS. Another whopper I've told on occasion comes up when people ask why I didn't become a commercial pilot after leaving the navy. The standard answer I give is that flying an airliner is like being a glorified, though well-paid, bus driver.   I chose not to pursue a career in commercial aviation because flying an aircraft when you have a major neurological issue is illegal. Rightfully so, the FAA tends to frown on pilots unable to pass the physical.   I don't fly because I have MS. My days of telling lies are over.

KENDALL GENESER

CHAPTER NINE
Fish in the Closet

We are all just salmon fighting our way up the river of life. Salmon swim until they can swim no longer. Their life's mission is life itself. And in their desperate, predestined struggle lies a lesson. They live until they die. I hope I can be like that. They swim as far as they can, for as long as they can. MS makes my stroke a little more challenging, but we all have our crosses to bear. We all struggle with some hidden maladies. Perhaps we haven't pinpointed those maladies ourselves just yet, but they're there, rest assured. We are all salmon. The measure of us all is our ability to overcome, persevere, and leave our mark.

Yet, that ability to overcome might be missed by the casual observer because disabled folks fight to hide their problems just as long as they can. I know this because I'm one of you. When we can't take it anymore, when it becomes blatantly apparent that something's got to give, we come out of the closet and step into the light. And man, it feels good. You can't drag someone into the light. They've got to come out when they're ready. But, for a lot of us, it's that distant bridge out there on the horizon. We are loath to cross it unless we have to. Sometimes it's the job. Sometimes we don't want to scare away someone who we think might be the "right one," and sometimes, it's just nobody's damned business. Regardless, it's a lonely life. The secrets isolate us and paint us into a corner. You end up working at a place for half a decade, and no one knows your name.

You can't run anymore, and you don't want people to notice. You limit verbal communications with others because you'll almost certainly trip on your tongue as it often has a mind of its own. You tend to stumble when you walk too far, so you limit trips to the bathroom since it's at the opposite end of the building. You don't stand around the water cooler, shootin' the breeze with your coworkers, because you can't stand for very long. People either think you have the drive of a super dedicated work fiend, or they just figure you for an asshole, but you're really neither. People don't know you. And, as long as you're willing to live in that closet, they never will.

Of course, the perceived risk is that when you step out, you will not pass GO but proceed directly out the door with an escort. What I've found in my few days out here in the light is that those of us living in closets give our bosses too little credit. Generally, folks will bend over backward to accommodate you. And who knows? Your story may serve as an inspiration to some of the other salmon in the river. It's a story that they can only hear clearly if you open the closet door.

CHAPTER TEN
"To Whom Much is Given…"

A friend of mine, who was recently named head coach of the local girls' HS basketball team, was telling me about a program run by our local National Guard. Corporations and teams of all sorts, from the college level on down, have the opportunity to run key members of the organization through the local base's obstacle course. This course is quite a bit different from the ones I remember running in Aviation Officer's Candidate School (AOCS), where success was measured individually. Army courses inherently require a significant amount of teamwork. You can't make it unless you work together. Courses require maximum effort from a whole team. People are carrying battery packs through swamps, that sort of thing. His next comment was telling. "It's a big deal because it tells you right away who your leaders are." I suspect that may be why organizations are lining up to run the course in the first place.

That whole exercise was designed to identify leaders in the group. That is what I used to be; it didn't matter what group. Any group I was in, I wanted to lead. In high school, I was the captain of the team and the president of the Student Council. In college, I was the captain of the team, the president of my fraternity, and the president of the Inter-Fraternity Council. I used to lead. That's what I did, but not anymore. Now I consider myself lucky if I can just keep up. That's hard to swallow.

I'm no longer at the front of the pack. I'm lucky to be bringing up the rear. It was initially athletics, and then it was student government. I was never really much of a leader academically, though I could hold my own. And as such, I logically assumed the next step, as a young naval officer, was to aspire to lead people in combat.

In my mind, I'm still a leader. Perhaps I've never been a good one, but a leader, nonetheless. But now I have to find a better way. Maybe I've been steered down this path less traveled (as Robert Frost's poem suggests) for something richer, better, and more important than the business of death.

I'm not sure that this is true. Truthfully, I sometimes wonder if I'm crazy in a delusional sort of way, but I choose to believe that there is some other plan for me that God has yet to reveal. I've *got* to think it. My sanity depends upon it. Permitting me to proceed along this track was only possible because of MS.

CHAPTER ELEVEN
Sweetest Rain

A common theme running through the stories of people with MS is that this wasn't the path they would have chosen, nor was it the life they ever would have imagined for themselves. No shit. Call me MOTO, for I am the Master of the Obvious, but life for someone that has difficulty walking is bound to be different. Who, after all, imagines themselves in a wheelchair? Yet if you consider only the physical limitations (i.e., that which is obvious), you're bound to miss a lot. They often say, "Into everyone's life, a little rain must fall." I've got to tell you; it's a friggin downpour here. But take a closer look.

I lost my career years ago. My children have grown up in a mostly fatherless home (admittedly, this is mostly my own damn fault). When I walk for a half-mile or more, I look like a drunken sailor by the time I arrive at my destination. I can't run anymore. As a result, I no longer enjoy the outdoors all that much if walking any distance is required. It's not like people hung on my every word, but now I'm pretty much irrelevant. No one ever asks me, "What do you think?" I used to worry about the effect of wind speed and direction at altitude and if predicted headwinds would be close enough to allow me to arrive alive. Now I worry about bladder urgency and bowel control. How's that for rain? Enough?

But Allah, or God, or Yahweh, or whatever you call the supreme being, had a different plan. I am uncertain of what that plan ultimately is, but I see myself as a potential "voice in the wilderness," which is what they called John the Baptist. I see myself as an advocate of some sort for my fellow human beings, especially those who happen to have multiple sclerosis.

I wanted to be a warrior, a great fighter pilot. Now I sit and write, and though I'm still searching, I think I'm finding my voice. Whether people will listen or not is still in question. But instead of a toolbox filled with power, strength, and intellect—nearly all of it wasted on honing my skills as a dealer of death and mayhem—God has made me weak so that the tools I still possess can be put to better use.

No, it's certainly not the life I imagined. I'm not standing on the hill at Yankee

Stadium about to throw the first pitch with 50,000 fans waiting breathlessly for me to begin the fall classic. I'm not looking at my radarscope as the enemy marshals its forces for one desperate surge toward a waiting armada led by me. Yes, it's raining. It's raining hard. But, upon closer inspection, it's not H_2O pouring out of the sky: it's raining honey.

Despite a difficult and rather cumbersome cross to bear, many blessings have been poured and are still pouring upon me. First, I have the privilege of seeing the absolute best in people. Time and again—from distant acquaintances to close friends to my children and, especially (constantly), from my wife—I've seen things that renew the spirit, quench a thirsty soul, nourish the mind, and restore one's faith in humanity. Second, the opportunity to tell you this story is a blessing in itself. It's the story of a man who thought worldly thoughts and measured his success with a worldly measuring cup, only to find that it was empty. It's the story of a man who has managed to let go of that worldly measuring cup and instead meter out true wisdom bought dearly.

KENDALL GENESER

CHAPTER TWELVE
Extraordinary

"There are no extraordinary men, only ordinary men in extraordinary circumstances." When Admiral William "Bull" Halsey uttered those words, he was talking about leaders of nations at or on the brink of world war. And, as tacky as it may seem—after all, nobody's shooting at me—it's the very best comparison I can manage. Dr. Brett Weber, a longtime fellow MS sufferer, considers himself a soldier on a mission. He writes, "My mission is not to be afraid or angry." He goes on to say that "Sometimes the mission does not seem possible." I agree. Sometimes it seems we're standing alone out here in no-man's-land, on an empty field with no ammo, totally exposed. But then I remember my brothers and sisters, and I know that I'm not alone. Legions of us "stand," assembled against this, our foe. I wonder if maybe my disease isn't part of some intelligent design that I can never fully understand. Is the war for which I so stupidly hoped long ago here right before me? Is my foe, my enemy, not some horde marshaling its forces on that distant horizon, but multiple sclerosis living within me, within my very central nervous system? I've been hankerin' for a good fight since I was a young man. Maybe God has placed a better fight before me.

What I've learned is that I am not unique. There are heroes and inspirational people all around you. Look in the mirror and—though I pray you'll never find out, for it's a heavy burden—you'll probably see one, hopefully incognito. They are virtually everywhere you look. It is a strange and terrible alchemy that makes heroism visible to the naked eye, but it lies deep within us all.

It takes two to Tango. To be an inspiration, and to remain positive and optimistic, requires the power of love. I know that one of the common symptoms of MS is depression. I've had my share of battles with it and will likely have more, God willing. One of the greatest cloaks of armor guarding against this is the love and support of friends and family. I know that it sounds cliché, but if not for the wonderful support of all of them—some in big ways (my wife), some in smaller ways (family and close friends), but all crucial—I'm not sure my life would be possible. Oh, who am I kidding? I'm sure my life would not be possible. It is my contention, then, that the other side of this equation, the other partner in this Tango of terror, whoever that happens to be at any given moment, has the more difficult task. While requiring help requires great patience, rendering help requires greater energy, an energy that only the purest love and kindness can generate.

Being a helper is more physically demanding, to be sure. They are responsible for getting the bags to the curb; they are responsible for maintaining some domestic semblance of order. In some cases, they help us dress. They are responsible for walking the dog, and the list goes on and on and on. But it is also more challenging mentally because you're constantly dealing with a fragile psyche. The person suffering from MS, though loath to admit it, doesn't like asking for help, doesn't want your pity, and, if you have some, you'd best keep it hidden. That is difficult. It takes an extremely high E.Q. (emotional quotient).

Good news for friends, family, and caregivers: unlike I.Q. (intelligence quotient), which most "in the know" deem innate, E.Q. can be refined, improved, and modified over time. I can't speak for others, but in my particular case, I've been privileged to watch E.Q. growing like weeds right before my eyes.

Maybe folks around me are just highly developed beings, but it seems that the level of comprehension, understanding, and empathy in those around me far outstrips the pace of my disease.

CHAPTER THIRTEEN
Dirty Little Secrets

The "dirty little secret" that scares the living hell out of me and, I would guess, thousands like me is that multiple sclerosis, like its distant cousin Alzheimer's, has a known impact on cognitive function. I am not talking about forget-your-name kind of stuff. I'm talking about more subtle things. You hopefully haven't noticed anything in written format. But you most certainly would notice if I were tasked with revealing these same sentiments to you verbally and face-to-face. Of course, you have no way of comparing the new me to the old one, so you might not have a sufficient basis for comparison. While I've always known that I wasn't the sharpest knife in the drawer, I can't help but notice a slight degradation in my own ability to reason. A witty turn of phrase that in the past I might have directed toward you now might fall on deaf ears when thrown my way. Simple math is more problematic. I was never a speed demon, but I do hold an MBA in finance, so presumably, I was, at some point, marginally capable of some quantitative heavy lifting.

There is some good news. Here it is: part of my need to write was not solely based on the long-shot hope of producing the great American novel or sharing the joy of flight. It was also the result of my own perceived necessity to keep my brain engaged. This constant exercising of my mental muscles, I believe, has helped to stave off the more insidious effects of the disease. In addition, since leaving the naval service, I've been employed as a stock analyst and am now serving a Midwestern utility firm as a risk analyst. So, although things happen at a slower pace—everything does—they still happen. And, more importantly, I'm doing all I can to stay sharp. I think.

That's the mental part. What about the physical? Well, if my cholesterol is any indication, my program to maintain some semblance of physical health is disastrous. Swimming was once my thing, but I'm not certain about that anymore. Staring at the black line is quite boring, and the place where I work now is not near a pool, which is why I stopped in the first place. I know, excuses, excuses.

THE GIFT

As I become less mobile, I've thought of taking up yoga. Sounds sort of weak to a former football player, but I am kind of weak, and I'm told you can make it as intense as you want. I'm sure the "sort of weak" comment will elicit a few responses. Feel free to direct your yoga wrath to my website. I do know that it greatly benefits range of motion, strength, and overall coordination. Water aerobics might combine the two exercise regimens and brings me to the next rather obvious point.

It is a simple law of physics that increased resistance reduces conductivity. Resistance increases as heat increases. MS, in a nutshell, is reduced conductivity between neurons. If you increase resistance in an already damaged system, strange things happen. You might fall. You might start dragging your left foot (I do that if it's too hot). That's why swimming or water aerobics is considered a great form of exercise for those of us who suffer the ravages of MS. You get a great workout while staying relatively cool.

KENDALL GENESER

CHAPTER FOURTEEN
Nick and Alex

At 3:25 p.m. PST on January 8th, 1989, our first son, Nicholas, was born more than a month ahead of schedule by emergency Cesarean section at Poway Hospital, CA. Poway is just up the I-15 from San Diego. It is called placenta abrupta, and doctors told us that a quarter-century earlier, both mom and baby wouldn't have made it. My wife lost a lot of blood. One of the few smart things I've done in my life was call an ambulance that day. Our son was almost born before I got there. He weighed just five pounds six ounces. He went to an incubator almost before he got the chance to meet his mother. She was sort of out of it anyway after losing so much blood. He looked like a frog. He was lying on his stomach with his little legs splayed out behind him like a frog about to hop.

It isn't a picture I'll live to forget. As I'm staring through the incubator at this sleeping frog, my firstborn son, I'm thinking about all of the things we'll do together. All the important things I'll be able to teach him and all the important firsts. I'm dreaming of that first fish, first haircut, and first foot race.

For the next seventy-two hours, I raced back and forth between Poway, where mom was, and San Diego's Children's Hospital, where my son was soon transferred. In the end, everything turned out okay, we think. My oldest is seventeen years old this January, so the jury's still out. Actually, he's a good kid. Unfortunately, he's dealt with a lot in his short stint on the planet.

Two and a half years later, our second child—also a boy—named Scott Alexander (we called him Alex at our oldest son's insistence) was born in Yokosuka, Japan. A tip to all prospective parents: don't let the eldest sibling— especially if he or she is just a toddler themselves—have a major role in picking names. Our second son, also delivered via Cesarean section, was not premature at all, weighing in at eight pounds and three ounces. We decided he was a keeper.

In the great nature or nurture debate, our two boys are, in essence, a social experiment. My oldest son's father was continually active physically. I took great interest in his advancement athletically. The kid could "hit a ton" at age five. He's the only kid I've ever known that would go off the high dive at three years of age. I wanted to instill the idea of "no fear" in a brave heart. Careful of what you wish for. He's given both his mother and me more than a few gray hairs over the last seventeen years.

As my disease progressed, I've done progressively less and less with my children physically. So much so that my youngest son was utterly denied the benefit of having an active, some might say, athletic father to show him the way of things. In other words, "Al the Pal" got screwed. He got short-changed big time when it came to having an involved dad. Now for the silver lining: as I've watched him grow and develop athletically—all on his own, by the way—I've watched him become a fine athlete despite, or maybe because of, my own lack of involvement.

It still sucks that I wasn't really there for him from a physical standpoint. I'm still grasping for other ways to be a part of their lives. But, much like me at their age, they're physical, outdoorsy, and athletic. If you can do something well, you should do it. Do it as much as you can for as long as you can. I'm not quite up to par as a runner anymore. I couldn't even imagine trying it. But sometimes, I still dream of gliding across the grass. I'm barefoot and carrying a pigskin rather haphazardly. If it were in organized football, someone (one of the coaches) would be yelling his lungs to leather due to my lackadaisical manner. But I don't hear. I'm too busy dodging fireflies and would-be tacklers as the goal line looms before me. Besides, this is sandlot football: coaches, what are they? I can hear my mom telling me it's time to come inside. And that dream reminds me that my sons need to enjoy their own graceful bodies just as much and as long as they can. By all rights, it is both fitting and proper to do so. Who knows what tomorrow brings?

But who am I trying to kid? Nick and Alex have largely grown up in a single-parent home. While I try to be the father my own dad is, I know in my heart that I've fallen woefully short. It's already way too late. He used to come home at lunch to play catch with me.

Can you imagine that? He's not rich. He's not important or famous, but I'll bet Saint Peter lets him pass when he's standing at Heaven's gate. There is absolutely no hope for me. I'm not sure that a healthy guy could do what my dad did if he wanted to have any kind of career. Actually, I do know the answer. If you have MS, you can have one or the other, not both, unless, of course, you're a friggin' genius, which I'm not. Color you stunned, right? There are only twenty-four hours in a day, and if you want to be a father, be one. It's taken me a few years to learn what is intuitive to most.

Meanwhile, my MS advanced, and my kids grew up without a father. That is to say, I was there, but I wasn't really there. Now, I'm sort of a non-entity, an inanimate object, like the furniture, in my own home. My oldest is a junior in high school. My youngest is now an eighth-grader. Part of me thinks that maybe MS was a blessing since it forced me to stay home so I could be there for my kids. The other part of me thinks my kids have been royally screwed because even though I was there, I wasn't really there for them.

Don't get me wrong, MS is my pretty decent excuse, but the truth is that my own head wasn't really screwed on straight. I committed the classic blunder; I forgot, for nearly a decade, what was truly important. I decided that if I couldn't fly jets anymore, I was going to take the world by storm in some other field of endeavor. I was going to wow society with something bigger than being a naval aviator. That never happened. Meanwhile, my boys grew up. But I got an MBA. I'm sure that'll impress Saint Peter when I try to gain admission at the pearly gates.

KENDALL GENESER

CHAPTER FIFTEEN
A Little Chin Music

I'm not a Communist. In fact, my very existence was once all about stopping Communists in their tracks, but I'm similar to Fidel Castro in at least one respect. When I was a young man, I wanted to play baseball for a living. From what I understand, the same was true of Fidel. Just think: if he'd had a little better arm, the world might be a better place. Even so, I suspect that a young Fidel was probably light-years better than I ever was, but nevertheless, we share this common bond.

My time around ballparks as a player ended when I was twenty-two years old, and, in later years, when my own boys were involved in Little League, I was able to put my skills to good use coaching various teams. Like Fidel, I lacked one thing: an arm. I did possess excellent control, though, and years later, my teams could hit the ball well because they had received a lot of live batting practice. I even coached teams for a few years after I was diagnosed. However, three or four years ago, I beaned a kid in batting practice. I used to be able to throw my fastball into a teacup at sixty feet. Yet I'd just hit one of my own players! I don't throw that hard, and this was Little League, so I was taking it easy anyway. It was that incident that finally convinced me that when I released the little cowhide sphere, I no longer knew, really knew, where it was going.

That's what MS does—you're in complete command of something, and then that something is completely taken from you. The only person that was really hurt by the incident was me. I doubt if the kid I beaned even remembers it. I won't ever forget it. This probably doesn't sound like a big deal, but I never threw batting practice ever again. A year or two later, I stopped coaching altogether. I know, cry me a river; find some other way to coach! Well, I haven't, all right? I think the best way to teach middle infielders how to pivot at second base is to show them. It's the same for nearly every aspect of the game. It's not like your lovely assistant is standing by to demonstrate the appropriate way to field a grounder. It's sad for me not to be able to teach the game I love, but it's unfortunate for a generation of young people too. (And I know what you're thinking: this guy's really full of himself—and maybe I am.) Of course, no one really knows what's been missed, how good it might have been. But I do.

KENDALL GENESER

CHAPTER SIXTEEN
The Job

Here's the deal: I'm not an invalid quite yet. I got a really nice cane for my birthday, but I don't use it except around the house. I still work. I'm not laying bricks or anything. I sit behind a computer and, as mentioned, carefully deliberate most events requiring movement of any sort. I tend to economize each and every motion. Still, I find myself trapped in this sort of tragic "do-loop." I was slow, to begin with, but MS makes me slower. As a consequence, it takes longer for me to complete my day's duties. A ten-hour day is sort of unusual in that it would be considered short. Yet long days (i.e., more mental and physical stress) make MS more rapacious. In a nutshell, MS makes my day longer, and long days make my MS worse.

By the time I get home at night, the kids are usually in bed, and I can barely drag my ass through the door in order to get up and do it all over again. Yes, I know there are hundreds of millions of us working hard to make ends meet. It isn't easy for anybody. I know that. Sometimes all of us are brutally dog-tired. But most folks with MS are brutally dog-tired every waking moment. By the time we get home, we're dead dog tired. I mean, "the house is on fire; I don't care, let it burn," sort of tired. I mean, "save yourself, go on without me" tired. In other words, the propensity to accomplish some other task once the workday is done is, for me, at least, not a realistic scenario. You see, work takes every ounce of my energy, and I have no gas left in the tank for anything or anyone else. That means that around the house, I am more like a piece of furniture than a parent.

Perhaps I can best put it into perspective this way: I've lived in my house for almost six years. Care to guess how many times I've mowed the lawn? Not once. I say again, zero, nada, zilch. I've never mowed my own lawn. Never have, and I doubt I ever will. My in-laws are kind enough to wrest that little chore from us. Now that my kids are old enough, sometimes they do it too. Some of you out there think MS has its advantages. Believe me; I'd rather be stuck mowing the lawn.

THE GIFT

The point is, at this stage, I can do my job or live my life, but I can't do both. Something's got to give.

CHAPTER SEVENTEEN
Telling the Boys

I left the Naval service in June of '98. We moved back home for the simple reason that we wanted to be near the people we love and who love us in case things went horribly wrong with my disease. Things have not gone terribly badly, but we did need help, lots of it.

In 2000 we moved to our current home, which is right behind the home of my in-laws. While some might consider this unfortunate, I do not. My wife's parents aren't intrusive or boorish in any way but instead are kind, considerate, and generous people. It wasn't long after our less-than-triumphant return to our ancestral stomping grounds that we told our sons of my disease.

I explained multiple sclerosis, its various forms, its common symptoms, and the way it had thus far progressed in me. I showed them my shots, which I had not previously displayed. In fact, I had taken great pains to hide them prior to this little announcement. At that time, I was doing AVONEX® (Interferon beta-1a IM). Their eyes got really big when they saw the length of an intramuscular needle. After a short explanation—remember, I'm talking to kids that are eleven and eight years old—I spent a few minutes attempting to allay any fears that I thought they might have. I assured them both that I wasn't dying, at least not anytime soon. I pointed out the fact that they hadn't even noticed much difference in me and that I'd already had the disease for several years. Of course, I knew that I was no longer chasing them across the yard, but the change had been so gradual that I don't think they even remembered a time when I did give chase.

I spent an inordinate amount of time instructing them on the rigorous chore of maintaining my confidentiality. At the time, I believed my physical condition was no one else's business. This, I now believe, was a great mistake. Placing the onerous responsibility of guarding my secrecy upon my boys was too heavy a burden to hang on children. What message does that send, anyway? I was an idiot, still deep in my own denial, and, almost as important, I hadn't come out at work or to the community at large. I wouldn't do so for several more years. To their collective credit, my sons, so far as I know, never divulged my condition to anyone like it would have been a big deal if they had. I'm coming out now, anyway. Now that I'm older and only a bit wiser, I believe that yoke was too heavy a burden. Had I to do it over, I would not ask them to bear that load.

CHAPTER EIGHTEEN
Making Time

In order to illustrate, I drew a hypothetical tombstone to signify my feelings at both the time of my diagnosis as well as during the intervening years. Multiple

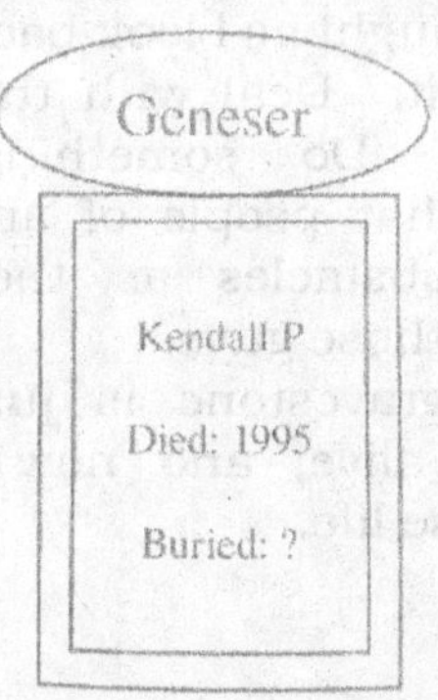

sclerosis ended life as I knew it. During the interim, I've been attempting, with little success, to take control of an impossible situation. I suppose that my considering a stem cell transplant is my desperate reaction to the situation. In essence, the period between then and now was me wasting time.

I don't want to leave you with the impression that this is simply one giant "pity pill," as my grandmother used to say, but I do want you to understand that I am a thinking human being and am fully aware of the range of possibilities and implications of both my disease and my choices to combat its progression.

A decade of my life was lost forever because I sat around feeling sorry for myself instead of creating a new niche for my new life. This effort is simply my affirmation of the necessity to begin anew. That's precisely what I'm doing: changing direction. It boils down to me being handed a truckload of lemons and deciding, finally, to make lemonade as fast as I can.

Life as I knew it ended a decade ago when a doctor told me flying was not an option. Now I have one thought as I look back on that period: get over it. Deal with this truckload of lemons. Do something. Philosophically, I know that people of any consequence overcome obstacles as they arise. I want to be one of those guys.

That hypothetical gravestone is just that, hypothetical. I'm alive, and now I choose to prove it. I choose life.

CHAPTER NINETEEN
Check-Out Time

Any sane, thinking human being facing terrible difficulty and a bleak prognosis in this life has thought about it. If they say they haven't, or they tell you it has never fleetingly crossed their minds, even for a moment, that person is telling a lie, or they haven't really been tested yet. It's sort of embarrassing to even write about it because I don't even feel like I've been tested hard enough to warrant such drastic measures. Part of me thinks I'm a weak and worthless waste of skin to even give the matter a moment's consideration. After all, there are people a lot worse off than me. I'm talking about suicide.

Before you rush to the phones to dial 9-1-1, before you check me into the hotel with rubber walls, please note that despite giving the matter serious consideration, I have no immediate plans for such a drastic act. I think a thinking person in such a circumstance considers it, hopefully fleetingly. First and foremost, despite a fighter pilot's bravado, I'm, at heart, a chicken. I don't want to die. Second, I'd want it not to be obvious. That implies nothing immediately recognizable from a forensic standpoint, like sleeping pills or eating my gun, or slashing my wrists. I'd probably want it to be some sort of automobile accident so my family would not be left suddenly destitute (life insurance, mine at least, wouldn't pay a dime if my death were ruled a suicide). And I don't blame them. Nor would I want my boys to live the rest of life with the stigma of suicide hanging over their heads. So that implies that I'd have to figure out something that would be ruled accidental.

I'm reluctant to include this little diatribe as I know it may delay the disposition of my estate—meager though it is—when I finally do meet my demise. It may even be challenged while snot-nosed insurance investigators attempt to uncover my C.O.D., as they say on the various CSIs.

But I, being of sound mind and questionably sound body, reject the notion altogether. I reject the notion not boldly or bravely but soundly nonetheless, on logical, philosophical, and moral grounds.

First, let us consider the logical argument. Things might get worse. I might suffer royally. My family might get run through the gristmill of MS, but twenty years from now, there might come a cure that totally restores me. Unlikely, perhaps, and I'm not about to pin my hopes on such an eventuality. However, if I off-ed myself tomorrow, that possibility would never be a part of my future. Life is full of surprises, but death is a permanent condition. I'm not willing to commit to that sort of irreversible solution. Philosophically it eliminates all other possibilities. There is no fork in the road when such a path is chosen. I'm not prepared to limit the few options I have. Chief among these is my need for self-expression. I can still sit up, I can still type, and though some may argue the point, I can still think. In a slight twist on the, "I think therefore I am" philosophy which Descartes first introduced way back in the 15th century, I do not think in order to prove that I'm alive, but instead want to live so that I may continue to think. My ability to communicate with the world after I'm dead is severely limited, despite what people see on television. As long as any one of these abilities remains, most especially the last, I'm not a waste of skin. My life is worth living.

Finally, I am a Christian. At least, I try to be. I believe in an intelligence that far surpasses our own. And, since I'm a practitioner of Christianity, I believe in the afterlife. That is to say, though I haven't been there myself, I believe in both Heaven and Hell. As such, I'd prefer to avoid eternal damnation, which people who've chosen an early checkout probably risk. I think I'd rather suffer a little bit right here. Pope John Paul II, during his own trial by fire, chose life with all its suffering rather than a quick and painless end. And, though it was intense toward the end, it was a lesson for us all. I'm thankful for the example and pray that I have that sort of courage because I choose life.

CHAPTER TWENTY
Seattle

As mentioned, I am contemplating a stem cell transplant to retard the progression of my disease. It has worked for many others, but, as you may imagine, it's somewhat risky. It can kill you. I wonder if this is simply another manifestation of me being selfish. Logically, I am willing to concede that it's a damnable choice. No one should ever have to make it. But the long and short of it is that my disease will progress, albeit slowly (hopefully), while I delay, or I can do it ASAP and miss three more months of my children's lives.

It gets worse. My "primary caregiver" is their mother, so in essence, this thing busts up the family during a critical point in their development. My wife has never been separated from her babies for more than one night. As a former naval officer, I certainly was, but this comes at a particularly difficult time. The holidays are right around the corner. Although we're not scheduled until the middle of November, the impending separation from our brood is already stressful, not to mention the fact that this is wholly elective. MS is not deemed terminal. The odds are quite good, but they're still odds. In effect, then, a stem cell transplant remains a gamble. The stakes are pretty high: life.

Still, the question is, what kind of life? At some point, I will likely deal with incontinence. Someday, conceivably, I won't have the manual dexterity to wipe my own ass. More than likely, a few years down the road, I'll be wheelchair-bound. Sounds frightening; those are, but a few of the many joys long-term MS patients may deal with. Still, it is life. Despite the glum prognosis— and eternal bliss aside for the moment—it beats the alternative. Oh sure, some people will flippantly argue that they would rather die, and it's damn well worth the risk. The people who say that are usually not actually facing it. Their perceived bravado is only a mask. It covers the fact that unless cornered, we'd all run away screaming like terrified little schoolgirls. I know I would, but unfortunately, I find myself in a corner.

CHAPTER TWENTY-ONE
Departures and Arrivals

On Sunday, November 13th, 2005, my wife and I traveled to Seattle, Washington, where I opted to undergo a stem cell transplant. The trip itself was largely uneventful, but a small part of me could not help but wonder if, as I said goodbye to my sons, I'd ever see them again. Yes, I know that is a somewhat melodramatic statement, but the fact is that an autologous stem cell transplant advertises a mortality rate of five to eight percent.

The flight went fine. It was our departure from Iowa and our arrival in Seattle that proved eventful. Without belaboring the tear-filled event, let's just say that our departure was fraught with enough lip trembling to register on the Richter scale. And after enough salt water to float, the QE2 had stormed down my wife's cheeks, we arrived in the Emerald City.

In Seattle, nearly half of all the stem cell transplants in the world are performed. Techniques for the procedure (both bone marrow and stem cell transplants) were first developed right here. The vast majority of transplants are for diseases other than multiple sclerosis. Indeed, the protocols for MS are still considered experimental. The perceived advantage of a stem cell transplant for MS is thought to be a reduction in the tempo of disease progression.

By suppressing—indeed eliminating, the immune system—the body's radical and wholly inappropriate response to myelin is eliminated. In other words, the hope is that by changing the immune system's response, by changing the immune system itself, the number of exacerbations and the advance of disability will be reduced. To liken it to the computer world, it's like rebooting the system. The body's immune system is rebooted, and although multiple sclerosis is still present—after all, there is no cure, as yet— symptoms should not reappear until a number of years commensurate with one's original diagnosis have passed. I was diagnosed at age thirty-four, so conceivably, if this works, I should be free from exacerbations until I'm sixty-eight years of age. That is why I've chosen to go forward.

As mentioned, there is some risk. More on that later.

We landed in Seattle to find its weather uncharacteristically clear, considering the season. Yet, despite the weather, we found that upon arrival, nearly everything that could go wrong did. Nothing too dramatic here, but when we landed, for a time, it was reckoned that my address book, the one containing all the important phone numbers, including the one to the Puget Sound Veteran Administration Medical Center's Transportation Office, had been inadvertently forgotten. It hadn't, and, after considerable wailing and gnashing of teeth, it was found stuffed in a zippered compartment of one of our seven—I say again, seven—suitcases.

This brings us to the next adventure: because we had seven bags, it was necessary for us to employ not one but two cabs. I had been out to Seattle in September in order to evaluate the VA's transplant program. Note: I'm quite certain that while I was evaluating the VA's transplant program, they were evaluating me. Needless to say, I was thoroughly impressed. And, because I had been turned down no less than four times by my insurance company at work, the Veterans Administration was really my only viable option.

In conjunction with the University of Washington's Fred Hutchinson Cancer

Institute, the VA houses prospective and current transplant recipients in one-bedroom efficiency apartments near downtown Seattle. In a demonstration of foolish ignorance, I mistakenly assumed that our accommodations were adequate. But upon arrival, my attitude was appropriately adjusted when I saw the place through my wife's eyes. The place that I thought suitable was, in fact, smelly, dirty, small, and inconvenient in every imaginable way.

However, our attitude was appropriately adjusted when we were introduced to the harsh reality of the Bone Marrow Transplant Unit on the fourth floor of the Puget Sound Veterans Administration Medical Center in Seattle, Washington. It's difficult to put your heart into bitching about one's accommodations when people all around you are fighting for their very lives.

CHAPTER TWENTY-TWO
Thanksgiving

A decade has passed since my diagnosis. I sit in our one-bedroom efficiency apartment in Seattle on Thanksgiving, the eve before meeting with doctors who will be discussing the particulars of the process, what to expect, and potential risks. Without boring you too much, an autologous stem cell transplant utilizing the BEAM approach will be employed to arrest the development or at least change the tempo of the progression of my disease. It is called BEAM for short because of the types of chemotherapy employed to alter or eliminate the body's immune system, the thought being that multiple sclerosis is simply the body's immune system gone haywire.

Specifically, immune cells called T-cells attack myelin (the fibrous sheath), coating nerves in the brain and spinal cord; doctors still do not know why. This part of the procedure is rather innocuously referred to as the Bone Marrow Conditioning Phase. The big news here is that nearly every one of the chemotherapies that make up the Conditioning Phase can be lethal.

Note: These drugs (which I'll list in a moment) are typically used to combat various cancers with great success. However, it is a desperate and, in many cases, final attempt to arrest an otherwise terminal disease. In my own case, while I believe my MS has gone progressive, it's not terminal. As such, the 5 percent risk of death that is advertised, and will certainly be discussed in the meeting, is, for obvious reasons, a big deal. It greatly complicates my decision process as it represents the tall pole in the tent. My vote, which I'll cast tomorrow by scribbling my signature on the consent form, is either a big roll of the dice or me handing over my future to the Almighty. I believe and hope it is the latter. Time will tell.

While our kids, back home in Iowa, celebrated Thanksgiving by attending a luncheon with all the fixins with their grandma and grandpa and dinner (again, with all the fixins) at their other step-grandma and grandpa's house, we went to our friend's home in Gig Harbor to do the same. Holidays with long-lost friends and/or relatives, especially if they happen to be gracious hosts, are a special experience. Our hosts, who shall remain nameless, are quite caring yet sensible about not overstepping the bounds of charity.

Fighter pilots and Iowans are proud people. I'm both, and thus have a hard time wrapping my brain around the idea of letting people help me. I suppose it comes down to the fact that any self-respecting fighter pilot believes that he should do for others, not have others doing for him; and to compound the issue, the Iowa part of my psyche is based on the notion that a people whose heritage stems from farmers/settlers on the windswept plains loathed asking for help because in that part of the world, one did for himself or died trying.

Of course, I'm improving on that score. While I detect an utter willingness to help in any way, I also detect a reticence to be too much, do too much. I wish I could bottle that and give some of it to my dad, who just about trips on himself to help in any way possible. But that's another subject. With our friends in the Pacific Northwest, the mix of kindness and humor is utter perfection. Moreover, the food was good. I'm certain they'll be appalled if they ever read this, as I know in my heart that they perceive their actions as good friends helping good friends and nothing more. Based on their always overwhelming hospitality, I'm inclined to think that perhaps they're right.

CHAPTER TWENTY-THREE
Sew What?

On the day after Thanksgiving, I signed the consent form authorizing the commencement of my autologous stem cell transplant. The protocol for my procedure is called BEAM, so named for the four types of chemotherapy employed in the conditioning phase of treatment. These are BiCNU or carmustine, etoposide (VP-16), cytosine arabinoside (Ara-C), and melphalan. The procedure, now used experimentally in the United States, was originally developed in Europe. The University of Washington's Fred Hutchinson Cancer Research Center has conducted an extensive study concerning multiple sclerosis using the BEAM method to understand better the effects of autologous stem cell transplants on the long-term progression of MS.

Many consider the procedure more aggressive, from a conditioning standpoint, than is necessary, and, as such, cutting-edge procedures have significantly modified the conditioning phase of a stem cell transplant. In other words, some on the cutting edge are backing away from BEAM. Why? Because the BEAM method uses forms of chemotherapy that are often used in treating other diseases and many in the world today are looking to less aggressive forms of conditioning to prepare the body's immune system for transplantation for multiple sclerosis.

The obvious question to ponder is why I would opt for this particular regimen when we appear to be on the cusp of better methods. Insurance companies still consider stem cell transplants for MS an experimental procedure. A program well underway at Chicago's Northwestern Hospital was rejected on four separate appeals/applications by me, using my work's health insurance provider. That is what brought us to Seattle. As a retired military officer, I decided to check and see if the VA would help cover the cost to do my stem cell transplant in Chicago. The process involved a letter-writing campaign to various politicians and the VA system itself.

Eventually, those letters found their way to decision-makers in DC and, specifically, the VA system. Their answer was short and sweet, basically noting two things: 1) that they would cover the cost of my stem cell transplant but 2) that the VA's Puget Sound Medical System, in association with the University of Washington's Fred Hutchinson Cancer Institute, was fully capable of performing the procedure and in fact were currently ensconced in studies that explored stem cell transplants and their effect on MS. A second reason for choosing the program at the VA's Puget Sound Medical Facility is one of expedience.

Any delay in treatment while I fight for what is perceived as the very latest in treatment offers an increment of time in which an exacerbation may significantly change my level of disability. That, in a nutshell, is why I choose to act. That is why my wife will spend an extended period in the Pacific Northwest, far away from our children. I've mentioned this previously, but about half the stem cell transplants in the world happen in Seattle. Although most have been for other diseases, experience is not solely limited to various cancers when you include previous studies at Fred Hutchinson. That said, so far as the Veterans Administration is concerned, I'm the first.

The day after I signed my consent form, I began receiving G-CSF subcutaneous injections. G-CSF (Growth Colony Stimulating Factor, or filgrastim) is a type of medication that stimulates the growth of stem cells within the bone marrow. Humans grow stem cells continuously within the bone marrow throughout their lifespan, and the growth factor simply stimulates growth at such hyper-levels that stem cells end up in your bloodstream. When counts are high enough, the stem cells are harvested in a process called apheresis. These are frozen and then given back to you after a conditioning regimen (read: chemotherapy).

Obviously, an autologous stem cell transplant for MS is predicated on the successful harvest of stem cells within one's own immune system. There are more than a few Colony Stimulating Factors that have specific intentions with regard to the outcome or disease that they are attempting to stimulate or fight. Other Colony Stimulating Factors include Interleukin-11, designed to accelerate platelet production; Interleukin-2, which is designed to develop killer cells to fight tumors more directly; Thrombopoietin (TPO) is a CSF designed to foster platelet production; Erythropoietin (EPO) aides in the production of red blood cells; or FLT-3 ligand, which is meant to stimulate the production of immature stem cells.

As mentioned, I'm given G-CSF in order to stimulate stem cell growth within the bloodstream. The brand most commonly used within the VA system is Filgrastim or

Neupogen®.　　Various　side　effects　are associated　with　these　Colony　Stimulating Factors.　G-CSF will often cause bone pain and, as a result, common painkillers, such as acetaminophen, Tylenol® (or Tylenol® #3, essentially Tylenol® and Codeine) are often prescribed to minimize the side effects of G-CSF.

Chapter Twenty-Four
Reap It

On November 29th, 2005, we were notified that my CD34 count was sufficient to begin harvesting. CD34 is the specific measure of stem cells within the bloodstream. It's measured in parts per million x 106 kg of your weight. I did G-CSF for four days. That's three subcutaneous injections per day for four days. My count began at one. On November 27th, 2005, they went to two. On the 28th, they had jumped to 75. When we got the call—on the 29th, when my stem cells were harvested at the University of Washington's Fred Hutchinson Cancer Research Center— my counts were around 111. I received my final injection of G-CSF at 0600 that very morning.

At 0830 November 30th, 2005, I began the harvest of stem cells at "Fred Hutch," as it's known for short. Harvesting of stem cells, more correctly referred to as apheresis, is accomplished by withdrawing blood from one arm and circulating it through a machine that separates the blood into various striations, removing certain components (in this case, the stem cells) and then returns the remains to the patient (that's me) in the other arm.

Large needles are plugged into veins in each arm. One is for outgoing, and one is for return. During the procedure—three to six hours—you've got to hold still and keep your arms straight. You're not supposed to sit up or anything. Have you ever tried to scratch an itch while keeping your arms straight?

I remember flying seven-hour missions over Iraq and returning to the ship, having not used a "piss bag." That was then, and this is now. Those commercials on television describing issues associated with bladder urgency—well, let's just say I actually listen to them now. Though MS has not rendered me incontinent as yet, I find that as life progresses, I don't stray far from bathrooms. Knowing that the apheresis is likely to approach my urinary tract's limit of endurance, I'm already considering the necessity of a massive relief effort before I begin the process.

I do my best to allay my concerns by discussing the potential looming snag with Jackie, our nurse, but she nonchalantly waves them aside, noting "that having to relieve oneself during the procedure is quite common." She doesn't go into great detail concerning the various methodologies used to combat this common difficulty, nor do I really ask. Though in retrospect, I noted the all too kind smile she flashed at my primary caregiver (my wife) as she made her exit.

At two hours, thirty minutes, and after several inquiries into when I could unplug, I received the welcome news that 1) the harvest looked good and 2) only about twenty minutes of the procedure remained. I can make it, I remember thinking. By now, the procedure had become a form of torture; my nose itched, my primary caregiver was snoring in the easy chair near my bed, and there was a porcelain-chipping wiz about to erupt from somewhere in the nether regions just below the sheets, when Jackie added the exquisite little twist, "Twenty more minutes and then about five minutes of flush with a saline solution."

So close and yet so far; sound the alarm General Quarters, General Quarters, all hands man your battle stations, walk, don't run, up and forward starboard, down and aft port. "Jackie?"

She'd seen that look before and graciously finished my sentence. "Not sure you can make it another twenty minutes?" she asked.

I nodded.

"I'll get you a urinal," she said and left the room.

Without descending into the sophomoric machinations of a blow-by-blow description of the ensuing relief effort, I will say that with the stalwart support of my long-suffering caregiver (Sherri), we successfully negotiated this minor speed bump.

Jackie, the RN, flushed my system with saline solution and then disconnected me from the machine. Although there were huge needles stuck into each arm, the most painful part of the process was the removal of the tape holding the needles in place.

During the process of relieving my bladder, Jackie took time to order me lunch. It was roast beef on rye with a tasty vinaigrette salad; a few stem cells for a free lunch—not a terrible trade.

CHAPTER TWENTY-FIVE
Inspiration

While this little treatise on the trials and tribulations of living with multiple sclerosis has proven thus far therapeutic, it has suddenly dawned on me that the whole point of the new me is not me at all. The point is derived from the title. I have the unique privilege through my disease to discover what is right and good. What prompts this rather obvious revelation has nothing, I say again, nothing to do with MS. Like some grand canal, MS has simply diverted my path in such a way as to allow me to see real courage, grace, and peace on a gargantuan scale, and perhaps just as important, I am honored to bear witness.

On the fourth floor of Puget Sound's Veterans Administration Medical Center, like at many medical centers worldwide, there is a Bone Marrow Transplant Unit. The vast majority—indeed everyone but the wife and I—has either been diagnosed, is the donor for, or is the primary caregiver of someone with some form of cancer. While the various treatments have improved markedly over the years, the long-term prognosis for most is not a rosy picture. For many in the program, a stem cell transplant represents the last gasp of hope in an ever-thinning list of treatment options.

Yet that less-than Utopian plane is the flower garden of human compassion. A smile, a remarkable level of optimism, and hope in the face of great odds are nothing if not awe-inspiring. It is the thing that producers and directors try to catch on the big screen. But that is not real, this is, and we're not forced to sit through fifteen minutes of commercials, previews, and reminders to turn our cells off, but I digress. I know a lady who's been through the process (a stem cell transplant); it didn't work. She's going to try again. I've been privileged to know brave people in my life, but I've got to tell you I ain't seen nothin' that compares to what I see every time I visit the unit.

CHAPTER TWENTY-SIX
A Remarkable Crucible

The uniqueness of my position never fails to amaze me. From this lofty perch, I've been allowed to witness the truly remarkable. Today, for instance, on December 5th, 2005, I had the privilege of witnessing my wife open a care package containing items from some of her coworkers. My primary caregiver is a teacher's associate at the elementary school near our home. Her package included chocolates (which she loves), popcorn (which she also loves), various candies, a sundry of lotions, and various local newspapers and other items.

All items were obviously selected with the greatest care and serious attention to detail. It was evident to even a social retard like me that someone had given great thought to each and every item in the box. I could see her eyes brighten with each item. It was a wonderful thing to watch. The teacher who sent the parcel had included a letter or picture from each of her students: first-graders saying they missed my wife or hoped her husband got well and that they missed her a great deal and hoped to see her soon.

She sat there on the floor, surrounded by many of the expertly chosen items. She didn't open the popcorn or munch on the chocolates. She didn't review the local news or look at the other contents; instead, she sat there and read aloud each of the first graders' letters, smiling and wiping the occasional tear from her cheek. It was then that I realized the magnitude of her sacrifice.

I had come to this realization long ago, but love truly does conquer all. It is love that enables ordinary people to do the extraordinary. My wife would obviously prefer to be elsewhere. Instead, she's relegated to handholding and caregiving for what could potentially prove a losing cause. That remarkable crucible is born with the greatest of ease. It's a splendid thing to witness.

CHAPTER TWENTY-SEVEN
Light at the End of the Tunnel

On December 9th, 2005, I began my conditioning regimen, more commonly referred to as chemotherapy. My first dose was BiCNU. BiCNU or Carmustine is not often used for various cancers but is thought highly effective where MS is concerned because it is known to penetrate the blood/brain barrier. Since many medications do not penetrate that wall, their efficacy is often thought to be limited. BiCNU represents the "B" in the BEAM protocol. One of the most notable things about BiCNU is that alcohol is used as a thinning agent to ensure proper viscosity. The dosage is dependent upon weight— in my case, this equates to about three stiff shots—and it, of course, is fed directly into your veins.

While I may have found the notion of pure grain alcohol fed directly into my veins an exciting prospect back in my college days, the wisdom of age has tempered my passion for Everclear. Never mind the fact that I walk around seemingly somewhat buzzed anyway because MS affects my balance in much the same way as one too many drinks. Now I operate under the principle of all things in moderation. The luster of inebriation has dulled somewhat with age and good sense.

The next day, December 10th, 2005, I continued the chemo regimen; Etoposide, the "E" in BEAM, was administered by the ML, as was ARA-C, the "A" in the BEAM treatment course. Although I'm not feeling considerable discomfort at this juncture, with no real nausea or lack of appetite yet, it is important to note that this part of the regimen is scheduled to continue for four days. During the intervening days of Etoposide and ARA-C, the likely possibility of one or more of the following symptoms will materialize: I can anticipate that the faster-growing cells, such as those lining the gastrointestinal tract, hair, and nails, will die. In its brutally efficient way, that is what chemotherapy is supposed to do: kill the fast-growing cells that are cancer. Unfortunately, it also attacks some of the other fast-growing cells as well. Extreme sore throat, difficulty swallowing, nausea, and loss of accompanying appetite may result. Of course, the possibility of hair loss is likely as well.

The final part of conditioning (read: chemotherapy) is scheduled for December 14th, 2005, my wife's birthday; happy birthday, Sherri. It's called Melphalan, and it represents the "M" in the BEAM regimen.

On day zero of my autologous stem cell transplant, my stem cells will be re-infused with the stem cells that were originally harvested and then cryogenically frozen over at the Fred Hutchinson Cancer Alliance. At this moment, my immune system will be severely compromised (i.e., non-existent). Such a state is referred to as neutropenic and simply describes one's ability to fight off infection. Absolute Granulocyte Count, or AGRAN, describes the virility of one's immune system numerically and provides an indication of an infection. Neutrophils are part of the white blood cells and are produced in the bone marrow and enable the body to fight off various forms of infection.

Because this conditioning regimen was conceived with the notion of compromising (i.e., resetting) the immune system, as opposed to the more common reason, that of killing cancer cells, it can sometimes result in the development of other secondary cancers. One of the telltale risks is called Epstein Barr Virus, or EBV. This rare development, which occasionally happens after an autologous stem cell transplant, is similar to mononucleosis and can lead to lymphoid cancer, which usually develops one to five years out from the transplant itself.

The administration of ATG, used to shape CD34 selection and ensure blood cell grafting, may increase that risk. Of course, I should have been monitored throughout the process for EBV, but as luck would have it, I'm told that initially, this step was forgotten. The good news here is that there is no news. Tests for EBV are, after a brief respite, again underway, and if EBV is discovered, it will be dealt with quickly because it is the harbinger of lymphoid cancer. A fifth chemotherapy is then called for; the monoclonal antibody called rituximab.

CHAPTER TWENTY-EIGHT
Happy Birthday!

I got re-infused on December 15th. In an autologous procedure, one's own stem cells (in this case, previously collected and frozen over at the Fred Hutchinson Seattle Cancer Care Alliance) were reintroduced to my bloodstream.

Many refer to the occasion as your birthday, as living long-term without stem cells is not possible. On that day, at the prescribed instant, two people from Fred Hutchinson Seattle Cancer Care Alliance came in carrying a white bucket and a thing that looked like a hot dog warmer. The hot dog warmer proved to be the machine used to thaw/warm the cryogenically stored stem cells to a precise temperature for re-infusion.

On or about that day, I began growth factor G-CSF once again. At this point, I should mention that I was no longer religiously recording activities/medications as they were given, as I suddenly found myself a bit out of sorts. Conceptually, G-CSF is given in order to bolster stem cell growth at a rate that is much faster than what nature will presumably do on its own; this is designed to minimize the interval of time that a patient is neutropenic. Simply defined, a neutropenic state occurs when a low white blood cell count (specifically the neutrophils) is extremely low. The immune system, as a consequence, is also compromised, thus increasing the risk of infection. My stem cells, now re-infused via IV, are destined to grow via multiplication within the bone marrow. The packets themselves are simply two ridiculously small, completely clear liquids infused into the bloodstream via a syringe in an IV tube. The process takes about five minutes. It's not painful.

CHAPTER TWENTY-NINE
The Future

Density, destiny, or fate: do you believe in any one of these? Or, like me, do you believe in all three?

First, I believe you have to be a little bullheaded (read: dense, obstinate, stubborn) to ignore the naysayers and plunge headlong toward the prize, despite the fact that you have no business getting even this far on your journey.

Second, I think it's largely destiny or fate that determines one's path in life. While I recognize that the two conditions are diametrically opposed—after all, why be stubborn if your life is predestined? Upon closer inspection, I think of one's destiny as the channel stretching out before us on life's journey; within that channel, we have the freedom to shape our path. So long as we "keep it between the navigational beacons," as Jimmy Buffet says, our freedom of movement within that predetermined path is limitless.

As a consequence, one's level of obstinacy is, in my opinion, a necessary thing if one hopes to have some semblance of control in this life. Of course, that control is, in point of fact, largely an illusion, but the illusion is a necessity. We, as human beings, seemingly need to feel some semblance of control within our lives. It's why physician-assisted suicide is even an issue in some states. Terminally ill patients are grasping for that final bit of control in a totally out-of-control situation.

Yet the reality is that control is, again, in my opinion, largely illusory. In my particular case, for instance, there are a variety of really bad outcomes that did, or in many cases still do, loom rather ominously on my personal horizon. Examples of the bad stuff include failure to engraft, fluid overload, engraftment syndrome, mouth sores and diarrhea, organ damage, infertility, or the development of other secondary cancers (sometimes as long as twenty years after transplant).

Logically I know that I ultimately have little control over these potentially horrible outcomes. But a little whisper-thin ray of hope is that the "the glass is half full" part of my personality recognizes that perhaps my outlook has somehow helped to prevent some of the bad stuff. I have a positive outlook. In other words, I want to live, and I pray to the force where I believe ultimate control does, in fact, exist.

CHAPTER THIRTY
Seventeen

At seventeen years of age, I was the BMOC, as they say. The world was exceedingly small, and I was its king. Or so I thought. I'm sure no one else did. The point is that now my eldest son is seventeen and, like his father before him, he is—or at least thinks himself—a big man on campus.

What is unfortunate is that his kingship has been usurped. At a time in life when you know all the answers, are essentially indestructible, are a prime specimen of humanity, and should be enjoying each and every minute of it, you don't need someone in your immediate family to rain on your parade.

What I'm trying to say is that seventeen-year-old kids should enjoy their ignorance. He's not the king, nor was I once upon a time, but the delusion is wondrous. When you're seventeen, you should enjoy that cocoon. Slowly, if life is merciful, over your remaining lifespan, your eyes are opened. And you suddenly realize that you are a small fish swimming in what is, in fact, just a tiny tributary of this great big ocean.

The rather sudden loss of that blissful ignorance, at any age, much less when blissful ignorance is rightfully its strongest, is about as brutal as it gets. My stay in Seattle, my baldness, and the ravages of chemotherapy are but a few things which those who consider themselves invincible should not witness. It's a big thing to swallow at age seventeen, at that age when one should enjoy his or her ignorance.

Of course, my oldest son is someone who seems to understand the dilemma in which I found myself. The likely possibility that an MS exacerbation would advance my level of permanent disability was very real, and, as a result, further delay was also a risk.

CHAPTER THIRTY-ONE
Medication

During my stay in Seattle, four patients passed. One was due to disease progression, but the other three—and this is somewhat frightening—were the result of infections. Being in the post-transplant phase of my treatment, infections (viral, fungal, or bacterial) represent the main dangers of this particular phase. Today medical professionals closed the Family Room (the place where family members and caregivers typically hang out) due to a currently unidentified upper respiratory virus. Patients were instructed to remain scarce for the day as identification was made and the room was properly disinfected. These things serve to highlight the major risks that patients face post-transplant.

The greatest risk, and the one that kills most people in the program, is an infection due to various viruses, bacteria, or fungi. That is why post-transplant people are given a variety of pills. Often, they include Voriconazole (an antifungal), Acyclovir (an antiviral), and various other medications and supplements.

Without delving too deeply into the virility of specific medications, please note that individuals that have undergone stem cell transplants are living on the very thin margins of life itself. That razor's edge offers no slack, no mercy for being wrong. Medical professionals rely on terrible experiences learned at a horrific cost. Doctors and pharmacists have managed to administer and monitor pharmaceuticals in exact amounts. And they understand what works.

Life is a precarious proposition for us all, but if you happen to be consuming large quantities of medication dispensed from the Bone Marrow Transplant Unit at the VA's Hospital called Puget Sound, your life is about as precarious as your sanity allows you to admit. I myself am a medical mental midget when it comes to naming the various drugs that professionals may typically use—to great success, I might add—to combat the many hazards that may rear their ugly heads post-transplant. But, at the likely risk of foundering in the sea of medical minutiae, I note that I've spent—some may say wasted—

the last twenty pages or so attempting just that.

While I had hoped my stay in Seattle might shed some light on autologous stem cell transplants and maybe even highlight a role for them in the fight against multiple sclerosis, the primary purpose of this effort was meant to recognize or celebrate my own public disclosure of my disease.

CHAPTER THIRTY-TWO
All the King's Horses

My wife is scheduled to leave Seattle on February 19th. Her return is long overdue. We had originally anticipated her departing Seattle on January 30th. It will be Valentine's Day tomorrow. The worry when I embarked on this process, was that our family would fall apart. I'm here to tell you that it looks as though our worries were warranted. The wheels are falling off. Earlier this week, we were alerted via email that our oldest son's current grade in English literature was a D+ and that our youngest son has failed his last two spelling quizzes. Wait, it gets worse. Our youngest son was found to have alcohol in school!

When it rains, it pours.

My initial concern that my family might crumble under the strain of this procedure appears to be coming to fruition. This is a damnable circumstance. My wife is practically tearing her hair out. We're from the sticks in rural Iowa. It's not unprecedented that the cops visit the local junior high, but when they're going there to talk to your son, it's a big deal.

Meanwhile, I'm staying here because the doctors are reluctant to release me prior to a prescribed interval that minimizes the risk of Epstein Barr or some other virus or bacteria. I suppose that one sign of health is when one has the strength to bitch. The docs don't want us to leave prior to sixty days post-transplant. Incidentally, it will be sixty days tomorrow.

Our hope is that everything will turn out in the end, that we'll somehow manage to thread the needle, and that we'll all be home and healthy, having done no permanent damage to our children. This is perhaps a naïve sentiment, but it is one to which we all must hang on with all our might. We have to hang on to something. Our hope is that we can put everything back together (so far as our family is concerned) upon my wife's return. Needless to say, while part of me wishes I could be there to help, the other part of me does not envy her. She's managed to see her husband through the worst part of an autologous stem cell transplant, only to be tossed out of the frying pan and into the fire. The task of reestablishing order on the home front is likely to be leviathan. Based upon recent events, coupled with our extended stay in Seattle, I find the familial situation reminiscent of the plight of Humpty Dumpty.

In fairness to our kids, I should note that considering the hand they were dealt, our two young men have comported themselves in an exemplary manner. I know that sounds weird, considering, but had we gone home on the schedule we had originally envisioned, all would have been quiet on the home front. The possibility of some unexpected medical issue, which may have proven overwhelming for a VA hospital in Middle America, was what doctors here in Seattle hoped to avoid.

As I recount the difficulties faced by my family, I'm reminded of Maimonides, a Jewish rabbi of the middle ages. He said that "a man looks at his own fate or at what happens to his friend, or at the disasters facing the whole human race, and he thinks: this is decisive in the vastness of things." Yet the fact remains that my individual life and, for that matter, the life of my entire family is scant more than a blip on a rather vast timeline. While my life or death seems of great importance—at least to me, and hopefully to my family and friends—it's really not that big a thing in the great scheme of the universe.

"God's universe must be considered as one great whole composed of interrelated parts, and its majestic purpose is not the gratification of our puny selves." This narrow view—Maimonides called it "narrow parochialism"—is an apt description of my state. In a nutshell, when faced with the proposition of life or the alternative (death), sane organisms will fight to survive. And, so doing, those of us fighting to survive tend to look at our own fate and not consider the wider view. It is this state of desperation that has led me to come here, despite any personal risk—and this is the selfish part—to our two children. This, in a nutshell, is why we're concerned. We're desperately hoping that my wife's return to Iowa will cushion Humpty's landing.

CHAPTER THIRTY-THREE
"One Small Step for Man..."

The powers that be have cleared me to return home, finally, on March 3rd. My wife has been back home for a few days and has had little downtime. As you can probably imagine, being away for three months has left a gaping hole in the fabric of the universe, at least so far as our family is concerned. Though loath to admit it, our sons need the love and guidance of their mom. The gaping hole her absence creates is much bigger than I ever imagined. What I've come to understand is the monumental impact she has on everything that she touches.

I don't mean to imply that she's perfect or anything—she makes mistakes, lots of them—but what I thought I knew before, that her presence in the life of our family is important, woefully underestimates reality. Now I know that she's the glue holding us together.   She's the gravity holding us earthbound. If not for her, we'd surely fly off the surface of this planet and find ourselves floating in space. I think if she had not gotten back home when she did, my kids might have spun off into oblivion.

But she's just one person, utterly magnificent, but one person, nonetheless. I should take a moment to acknowledge that there were a whole host of folks involved directly with this extraordinarily complex operation. Family, friends, and neighbors were integral to the plan's success and, by definition, are the finest examples of humanity you'll run across.   My in-laws watched two adolescent boys, at best a difficult proposition, ran an extra household in our absence, and as if that weren't enough, my mother-in-law actually acted as my primary caregiver, spelling (not sure who spelled who) my wife during the latter part of February.

Countless friends were watching over the place, and any skullduggery perpetrated by our offspring was met with close scrutiny. Friends and relatives took one or both of our kids to spell my wife's parents almost every weekend. In the end, it all worked. I'm home, and barring some infection, I'll live to tell about it. I liken this scheme of mine to President Kennedy's call for a moon shot in his first inaugural address. I wonder if he understood just how difficult his call would be, that it would take millions of man-hours, piles of dollars, and nearly a decade to bring his sentence to fruition.

I can't comment on a sentence in an inauguration speech that occurred before I was born, but I can tell you that I damn sure underestimated the cost of an autologous stem cell transplant. Oh, I understood the economic impact, what would be required of me personally, the risk, and the difficulties, but I just didn't realize the magnitude of support required by so many. I'm reminded of Hillary Clinton's book *It Takes a Village*, written when she was First Lady. I assure you, it takes a village of considerable size to send one person to Seattle for medical treatment. But the analogy that I prefer is one of an astronaut. Recall that early on in this work, I tried to convince you that I never wanted to be an astronaut.

Well, that is mostly true, but not completely. Like President Kennedy's sentence so long ago, my announced intention threw into action an unanticipated apparatus of support. A myriad of folks, some contributing with financial assistance, helped get one guy a stem cell transplant in Seattle. While it's not "one large step for mankind," it is, in my opinion, an equally beautiful thing. And it is greatly appreciated.

KENDALL GENESER

124

CHAPTER THIRTY-FOUR
Dear Oprah

Dear Oprah,

My wife deserves something very special. She raises our kids, runs our home, works full time, and has ample love to spare. It's awesome. As if that weren't enough, she was my primary caregiver this winter (2005-2006) when I underwent a stem cell transplant. Needless to say, when we exchanged vows—the part about "in sickness or health"—I'm very glad that at least one of us paid attention and took it to heart.

In 1985 the girl I love said yes, and made, what I think, was an ultimately bad bargain. Had she known then that she would get dragged across the globe, require not one but two C-sections, endure long separations, and live her whole life in less than opulent conditions, only to age before her time and be awarded a sick husband to live with and care for to boot, living life as a largely single parent, I wonder if she would have still chosen me?

The short answer is, I believe, yes. If not yes, then she's managed to convince me. She's put a brave face on what, undoubtedly, is a horrid predicament. As Barry Manilow might say, she's hopefully "made it through the rain" and come out the other side to "find herself respected" and loved all the more by everyone for her trials and tribulations.

I don't know if there's anything here, but if you ever do a show where you give women who got a raw deal some pampering (maybe some kind of Valentine's Day at a spa or something). I hope you'll consider my wife a potential guest. She deserves much more than I could ever give her, and that's where you hopefully come in.

Thank you.

CHAPTER THIRTY-FIVE
Overcoming the Status Quo

I've spent the last several pages trying to convince you that I'm generally upbeat; that I've come to terms with MS, albeit slowly; that I'm a "glass is half-full" kind of guy. I've happily used three of the five drugs mentioned below, but...

There's another way to think about what I believe is a promising, though still risky, treatment. Stay with me here. Drugs like Avonex, Beta-Seron, Copaxone, Rebif, and others in the pipeline, including Tysabri (which at this writing has not yet received FDA re-approval after being voluntarily removed from the market), are all great drugs designed to combat the severity and/or decrease the frequency of exacerbations. In other words, they combat the symptoms of MS, not MS itself, thereby reducing cumulative disability over the long term.

Now for the cynical part: drug-makers like Biogen, which makes Avonex and is the major partner (along with Élan) in the production of Tysabri, are major contributors to the National Multiple Sclerosis Society, MS World, and others. The obvious public view of drug makers, as well as the NMSS, is that they want to end the disease. And, of course, that is likely the truth, but the rather cynical fact of the matter is this: I take none of the aforementioned drugs currently.

As it stands, though MS still exists within me (I was originally diagnosed at age thirty-four), in theory, I'll be sixty-eight when MS rears its ugly head again. If my autologous stem cell transplant worked, I'd be disease-free for the next three and one-half decades! To be more precise, if it worked, I wouldn't even look at Copaxone, Avonex, or Tysabri for another thirty-four years. That loss of sales is insignificant when we're talking about one case. But imagine the world if people began flocking toward similar forms of treatment. The loss of sales would potentially be leviathan for drug makers. A portion of those funds would have gone to support NMSS and others.

The cynical view is that drug-makers aren't hoping for a cure so much as to manage the disease with—oh, by the way—daily or weekly (monthly in the case of Tysabri) injections/infusions. And those treatments are expensive.   Secondly, the National Multiple Sclerosis Society will resist the idea of masses of people opting for stem cell transplants because it will cause a major source of their funding to dry up.

Admittedly that's a cynical view, or perhaps we can chalk it up to "the law of unintended consequence"; I'm not sure I myself believe it. Time will tell.

KENDALL GENESER

CHAPTER THIRTY-SIX
A Delusional Conclusion

Maybe it's true. Maybe when one is faced with a currently incurable and insidiously progressive neural disorder, one has to be slightly delusional if one hopes to paint even the thinnest slice of sunshine on his or her personal horizon. It is said that someone once asked Charles de Gaulle if he was happy, and his response was something to the effect of, "What do you think, I'm stupid?"

Well, maybe I am—stupid, that is—but I believe there is another way to look at it all. I'm of the opinion that we have to grab hold of the gifts we've been given in this life and leave our indelible mark on this earth. I choose to accept this thing I have and embrace it. I choose to be thankful for my life and to celebrate it. I choose to share. Through MS, I've been gently cajoled down a very different path than I ever envisioned. Without making you puke, I hope you've been convinced that life, not despite MS but because of it, is a gift.

There are perfectly healthy people all around us that are so uncomfortable in their own skin. I wouldn't wish that on anyone. They crave something they'll never live long enough to find. These spiritual toddlers walk around on the earth for seventy, eighty, or ninety years and never ever strike on the things that really matter. They never know how good making others feel good can be. They never learn what their true gift actually is. They go through the motions, and then, if they are lucky, they live just long enough to regret not that which they've done but that which they've failed to do. I've done my time as a spiritual child. I was meant to be a fighter pilot and a warrior like I was meant to have a hole in my head.

Now I've been given this second chance, this gift from God, to do something that matters, really matters. I don't know for sure what that something is just yet. I've spent nearly a decade in the morass of secrecy. For all I know, this may be something I was meant for. I'm okay with that. While I hope for a cure and will actively scramble to delay the onset of further disability—my trip to Seattle is evidence of that—I realize that while multiple sclerosis has been physically debilitating, it's been mentally and spiritually liberating. It has been a gift.

P.S.

Some years ago, I read Admiral Jim Stockdale's book *Thoughts of a Philosophical Fighter Pilot*. Note I highly recommend it. In it (pg. 124), I found this poem. It was discovered in a Civil War POW camp, unsigned. It has become my new favorite:

We asked for strength that we might achieve;
God made us weak that we might obey.

We asked for health that we might do great things;
He gave us infirmity that we might do better things;

We asked for riches that we might be happy;
We were given poverty that we might be wise.

We asked for power that we might have the praise of men;
We were given weakness that we might feel the need of God.

We asked for all things that we might enjoy life;
We were given life that we might enjoy all things.

We received nothing that we asked for;
But all that we hoped for.

And our prayers were answered. We were most blessed.

The End

P.P.S.

Truth in advertising: so here I sit astride this beast called Multiple Sclerosis. Like anyone combating this disease and not letting it win, I just pull my hat down and hold on for dear life. In August, I went back to Seattle for an MRI and a checkup. I was ecstatic when the Neurologist told me there were no new lesions. The transplant worked! Right?

Not so fast. I penned these words in November 2006. This is an update of sorts just before my little work goes to print. And I'm having a minor exacerbation. I'm doing a short course on IV steroids. Recall that when I signed my life over to the Bone Marrow Transplant Unit in Seattle, WA, doctors were quick to point out that the effort is designed – not necessarily to stop MS in its tracks, although that's what everyone hoped – but to change the tempo of disease progression. The jury's still out, but despite recent events (i.e., my current flair-up), I choose to believe that my transplant was successful. I'm sure I believe that for the sake of my own sanity, but there are some pretty compelling supporting indications inclined to bolster my optimistic, some might say foolish, outlook.

First, my current exacerbation does not seem as severe—so far—as those previous ones. Second, before the transplant, I believe that I was on the verge of going progressive. Secondary progressive MS is characterized by exacerbations coupled with cumulative disability. In other words, the trend is downward. I had exacerbations every three to six months. It has been more than a year since my previous one.

Also, though I plan to talk to my neurologist about this, my current shot is not Copaxone, Avonex, Beta Seron, or Tysabri. It's nothing, nada, zip, zilch. A possibility I am going to consider is one of these in combination with my autologous stem cell transplant. Finally, and most important—in my opinion-I'm alive. I'll get back to you with annual updates on how it all works out if you buy the book. Thanks.

PICTURES

My commissioning as an Ensign (E-01)
September 27th, 1985

Me holding Nick in front of the
USS Constellation.
Just got back from NORPAC in 1989

Me in San Diego at NAS Miramar in 1990

Aileron, my Golden Retriever, at
One year old, 1988

Nick and Sherri watching me fly in from my
first cruise in 1990

Neighbor (Patrick) with my sons, Alex and
Nick, in Fallon, NV

Alex is carrying a pumpkin in
Fallon, NV, in 1994

Me fishing for silver salmon in
Alaska in 1994

Me flying an F-5E in 1995

Me flying an F-5E in 1995

Sherri and I in front of a VFA-127 F/A–18A
Decommissioning of VFA-127

Sherri and I at an awards banquet in 1996

Older Nick holds a rainbow in
the Black Hills in 2002

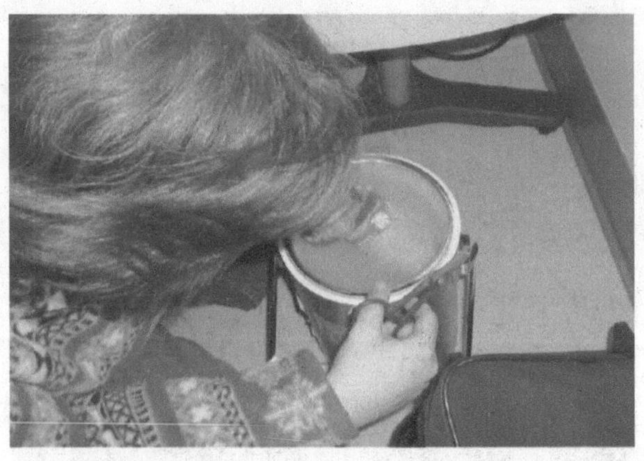

One of the nurses fishing for my
stem cells in a cloud of nitrogen

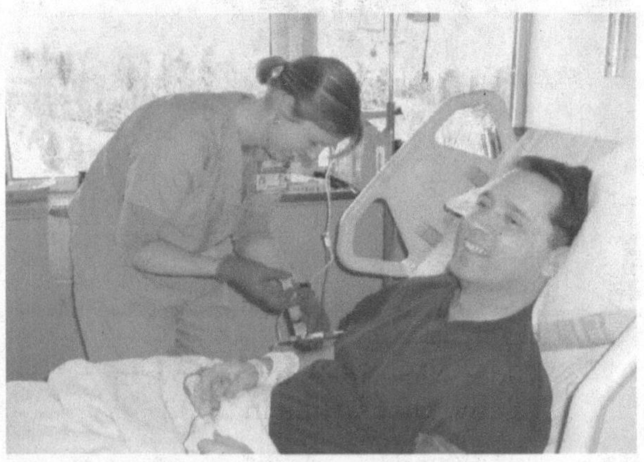

Allison (my nurse) giving me
my stem cells back

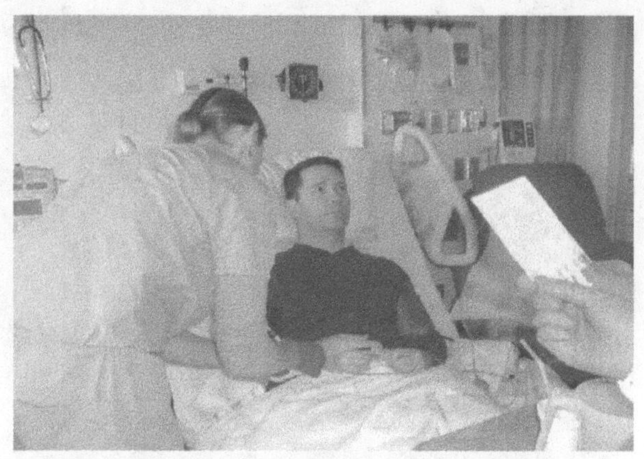

Me watching TV while nurses fuss about

Me, Sherri, Nick, and Alex, Christmas 2005,
in my hospital room in Seattle

The family, with me starting to go bald

Mom and the boys, Christmas, 2005
She hadn't seen them in a few weeks.

Several of the principals running the unit are pictured here. Three doctors, a dietician, a nurse, a sociologist, a psychologist, and a pharmacist.

work. The author receives the latest medical treatment and openly discusses it in his quest to come out of the closet concerning his medical condition. He recounts his autologous stem cell transplant and does his best—in layman's terms—to explain the procedure, its risks, and its likely outcome. The result is this sad, happy, funny, and sometimes frustrating account of coming to terms with the challenge.

Note: The author is not a doctor but a layperson and knows there are few pat answers with M.S. Please consult your physician before making any medical decision based upon this work.

ABOUT THE AUTHOR

Kendall Geneser is a former naval aviator and 1993 graduate of the Naval Fighter Weapons School. Now medically retired due to a diagnosis of Multiple Sclerosis, he has cast about for a number of years searching for meaning and purpose in his life. He has been a stock analyst, a risk analyst, and an insurance agent. In his first memoir, he has found the one thing that truly matters.

After his diagnosis in 1997, thus ending his military service, Kendall found himself a young father and husband battling mounting depression and the relentless progression of physical disability. The former Top Gun graduate was adrift in a world devoid of purpose, or so he thought. Yet, there was another way to think about the tragedy that ended his flying career. Perhaps MS was a gift.

Kendall holds an MBA from the University of Iowa. He is the author of several works of fiction written under the pen name of Max Cioux. He is happily married. He and his wife have two grown sons.

A decade later, Kendall published his follow-up memoir entitled *"GROUNDED: A Different Kind of War."*

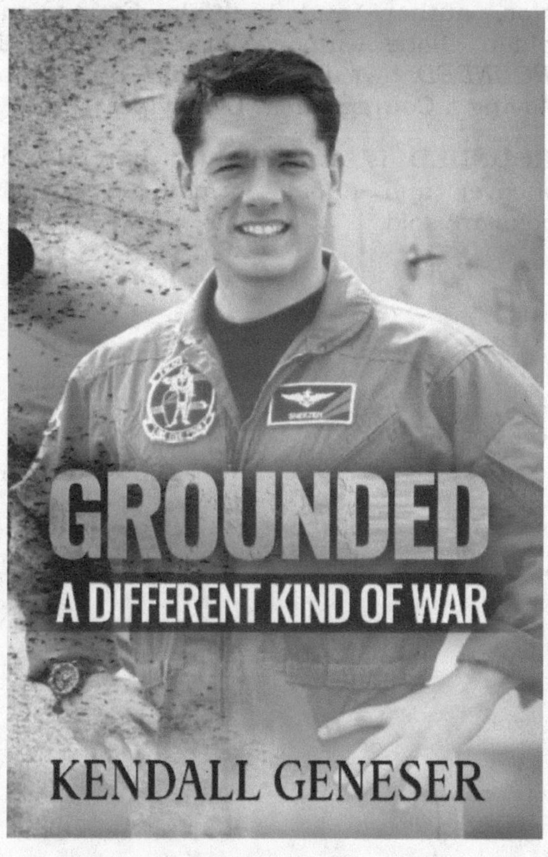

GROUNDED details the journey of how his life changed after The Gift was published. Kendall went from "what's in it for me" to "what I can do for others." He details the events and the bitter pills he had to swallow to get him from the former way of thinking to the latter.

Actor, author, and multiple Emmy and Golden Globe winner Martin Sheen hails *GROUNDED: A Different Kind of War* as "Moving... Courageous... Deeply personal."

GROUNDED is available for purchase in softcover and eBook formats everywhere books are sold.

THE FIGHT CONTINUES
Why was GROUNDED written?

In Kendall's own words: "Quite simply, it's a memoir that details my personal faith journey, and to that, some will say, 'Big deal. Everybody's got a story. What makes yours special?' I was a Navy fighter pilot on top of the world when I was diagnosed with Multiple Sclerosis. Suddenly, I was scrambling to find meaning in my life. Sadly, a lot of people (especially men) define themselves by what they do instead of who they are.

There's a line in the movie "Top Gun Maverick"—which, as one of those guys, I dug the movie—but it's something like, "Fighter pilot is not something I do. It's who I am."

That's admirable, on the one hand, that sort of dedication and all, but it's also kind of sad. The first word out of the mouth of Jesus during his public ministry is repent. To a lot of folks, that sounds sort of preachy, sort of fire and brimstone. But it's not at all. All it really means is to turn around, go a different way, and choose a better path.

In my story, MS is the rather harsh medicine that forced me to choose that better path. I no longer define myself as a former Naval Aviator but as a Christian and a child of God. That, in a nutshell, is what *GROUNDED: A Different Kind of War* is all about."

In a world where faith is constantly under fire, Kendall is still fighting "A Different Kind of War." Words are powerful. Stories of strength in the face of adversity are powerful. Kendall can only do so much to fight the "Good Fight" by himself.

You can help. We all can help fight "The Good Fight." Through speaking engagements and book tours, Kendall continues his journey of spreading the word face-to-face with congregations, law enforcement agencies, and with those who proudly serve (or served) in our armed forces.

These things cost a pretty penny to coordinate, and the resources needed to fund these engagements are not always readily available. Here's where you come in. Concordis Publishing, the publisher of this very testimonial, will launch an ongoing crowdfunding campaign early in the summer of 2023 and will last until the snow begins to fly where Kendall lives in Granger, Iowa.

What will this campaign aim to accomplish, and who will benefit from your contributions?

Very simply, Kendall will continue to share his testimonial, and the beneficiaries are threefold:

- ***Mary's Meals:*** Mary's Meals provides life-changing meals to some of the world's poorest children every day they attend school.

- ***Tunnel to Towers Foundation:*** Since 9/11, Tunnel to Towers Foundation has been helping America's heroes by providing mortgage-free homes to Gold Star and fallen first responder families with young children and by building smart homes for catastrophically injured veterans and first responders. They are also committed to eradicating veteran homelessness and helping America Never Forget September 11, 2001.

- ***Ongoing Support:*** A portion of the funds from this campaign support the daily actions of Concordis Publishing and allow us to continue our efforts to share these stories together.

crowdfundr

What is crowdfundr?

Crowdfundr is a crowdfunding platform that is quite different from the others you may have known about.

- Firstly, *crowdfundr* does not—repeat, does not—retain any percentage of the money contributed.
- Secondly, *crowdfundr* is tailored specifically for creators and authors like Kendall and Concordis Publishing.
- Lastly, *crowdfundr* is a team of twenty professionals who work closely with us to ensure that we have maximum exposure and outreach.

Crowdfundr is a relatively new platform. Unlike Kickstarter and other crowdfunding platforms, their entire team is completely dedicated to providing us with the tools and resources needed to ensure our success, no matter how long it takes and no matter how little (or how big) our campaigns.

What's in this for you?

This isn't just about money. Please take a moment to read the five words above again. "This isn't just about money." It's easy to simply ask for donations.

There are different "levels" of contributions, and each has a reward or "perk" that you can choose based on your level of contribution. They range from a simple monetary contribution of $20 at the entry level to the rather lofty "perk" of booking Kendall for a speaking engagement at your congregation, law enforcement seminar, or a military function for $5,000, $7,500, or $10,000 (depending on location) at the high end. Regardless of your contribution level, there is something in this campaign for everyone, including (but not limited to) the following:

- eBook version of *GROUNDED: A Different Kind of War.*
- SIGNED copies of *GROUNDED: A Different Kind of War.*
- eBook version of *The Gift.*
- Softcover version of *The Gift*
- SIGNED softcover versions of *The Gift.*

- Your name in the "Acknowledgments" sections of future editions of *GROUNDED: A Different Kind of War* and *The Gift.*
- An in-person speaking engagement by Kendall Geneser at your congregation or function.

New "perks" or "rewards" will be added to the campaign as they become available.

The biggest reward is our thanks, and a thank you on behalf of Mary's Meals and Tunnel to Towers Foundation.

Where can you find the campaign?

There are two ways to find the fundraising campaign on crowdfundr. You can type the link below in your browser EXACTLY as it is listed, OR you can simply scan the QR code with your phone, and you will be taken directly to the campaign.

Here is the web link

(type the link exactly as it is written):

https://fnd.us/adifferentkindofwar?ref=sh_7
C8D61

Here is the QR Code

(scan with your phone's camera):